AMERICAN PREP

THE INSIDER'S GUIDE TO U.S. BOARDING SCHOOLS

Ronald Mangravite

Published by Mango Publishing Group, a division of Mango Media Inc.

Cover, Layout & Design: Elina Diaz

For permission requests, please contact the publisher at:

Mango Publishing Group
2850 Douglas Road, 3rd Floor
Coral Gables, FL 33134 USA
info@mango.bz

For special orders, quantity sales, course adoptions and corporate sales, please email the publisher at sales@mango.bz. For trade and wholesale sales, please contact Ingram Publisher Services at customer.service@ingramcontent.com or +1.800.509.4887.

AMERICAN PREP:
The Insider's Guide to U.S. Boarding Schools

Library of Congress Cataloging
Names: Mangravite, Ronald
Title: American Prep / by Ronald Mangravite
Library of Congress Control Number: 2017901656
ISBN 9781633534896 (paperback), ISBN 9781633534902 (eBook)
BISAC Category Code: STU000000 STUDY AIDS/General

Author Photo Provided By Bob Lasky

Front Cover and Interor Images: Jannis Tobias Werner/Shutterstock.com, f11photo/Shutterstock.com, EQRoy/Shutterstock.com, Joe Mercier/Shutterstock.com, and AN NGUYEN

ISBN: (paperback) 978-1-63353-489-6, (ebook) 978-1-63353-490-2

Printed in the United States of America

"*American Prep* is the most comprehensive and accurate book on the American boarding school experience I have ever read. Ronald Mangravite captures the many facets of a boarding school education with remarkable clarity. Without bias or agenda, he shows why boarding schools are a powerful educational model which prepares children from all parts of society for success as adults."

Thomas Sheppard,
Dean of Enrollment Management, Lawrenceville School

"As parents who stumbled upon boarding school as a viable alternative for our daughters almost four years ago, we wish we would have had a resource such as *American Prep* to better prepare us for the process. The insights on parenting boarding school students are invaluable to all families considering or already in the process of sending a child to boarding school."

Lia Yaffar-Pena,
St. Timothy's School parent

"American boarding schools are NOT what you see in the movies! They have evolved into inclusive, supportive communities while continuing to deliver the sort of academic and character-based education for which they have been renowned. Through candid descriptions of life at today's schools, and detailed road maps through the admission and financial aid process, Ronald Mangravite provokes what will be an eye-opening revelation for many people: an American boarding school education is both extremely appealing and surprisingly accessible."

Ian Gracey,
Dean of Admission & Financial Aid, Groton School

"This is a very thorough book and especially useful for international families. We have needed a book like this for decades; I wish *American Prep* would have been available when I went to school. Read it, then keep it as a reference…a treasure trove of information!"

Diego Munoz-Tamayo,
Thacher School alumnus, Choate Rosemary Hall parent, Deerfield Academy parent

"If *American Prep* had been available to us when we started our search, the road to boarding school would have been significantly less daunting. I highly recommend reading it and referencing it throughout the process."

Lisa Cloughen, Portsmouth Abbey School parent

"This book is so well-written it is ridiculous. The depth of thought that has gone into it is impressive; it is coming from a very centered place that will speak to the heart of any parent or child considering this particular road trip. I found it very moving as I reprocessed my own prep school 'career' in parallel with reading it…The examination of school costs and financial aid support is particularly illuminating."

Phil DeMuth, bestselling author, Forbes contributor, Lawrenceville alumnus

"Exceptionally comprehensive, *American Prep* is both a good read to familiarize oneself with U.S. boarding schools and a detailed reference guide to draw on throughout the boarding school experience."

Paul Sardina,
Culver Academy Alumnus and Parent

TABLE OF CONTENTS

INTRODUCTION	9
PART I - IS BOARDING SCHOOL FOR US?	14
CHAPTER 1 BOARDING SCHOOL BASICS	15
CHAPTER 2 BOARDING SCHOOLS TODAY	37
CHAPTER 3 BOARDING PROS AND CONS	69
PART II - THE SEARCH FOR SCHOOLS	86
CHAPTER 4 THE QUEST BEGINS	87
CHAPTER 5 YOUR FIRST SCHOOL LIST	123
CHAPTER 6 PHASE THREE - ZEROING IN	153
PART III - ALL ABOUT ADMISSION	170
CHAPTER 7 THE APPLICATION PROCESS	171
CHAPTER 8 FINANCES	191
CHAPTER 9 DECISIONS AND DEADLINES	207
PART IV - BOARDING SCHOOL LIFE	230
CHAPTER 10 WHAT TO DO AHEAD OF SCHOOL	231
CHAPTER 11 BOARDING SCHOOL PARENTING	243
CHAPTER 12 EXTRA CREDIT!! ADVICE FOR STUDENTS	261
AFTERWORD	301
ACKNOWLEDGMENTS	303
APPENDIX	306
INDEX	312
BIOGRAPHY	317

INTRODUCTION

Picture this...

It's early morning at an American boarding school. The dawn's light, filtering down through majestic old trees – maples, oaks and elms - falls gently on a vast circle of manicured lawn, bejeweled with dew. A small herd of deer grazes serenely along the fringe of the campus woods. Out on the river nearby, the crew team is completing a morning workout. Soon chapel bells will begin to peal, heralding the onset of the school day. Students will stroll forth towards ancient ivied academic buildings where their instructors await to begin the academic day ....

That's quite an idyllic scene, isn't it? But are boarding schools really like that? And how in the world does one go about finding out?

My first encounter with the boarding school world was hardly romantic; more like film noir. I arrived abruptly, sight unseen, due to family circumstances. My father drove me to the campus on a raw, rainy morning in early fall. I had one suitcase and a foot locker. I checked in at the administration building, we shook hands and he left. My boarding school life began.

The school was one of the well known ones, old and beautiful, but with an atmosphere as chill as the autumn wind. Despite this, many of the boys (for this was a single-sex school, as most were then) appeared to be having a grand time. These kids were fast friends, high spirited, enthusiastic about everything in school life, except perhaps the food and the daily chapel requirements. As a new boy, utterly clueless about boarding school culture, I was apart from this camaraderie. I struggled with my classes, and both feared and admired my teachers in equal measure. I felt unwanted and kept to myself, lonely and homesick.

Over time, things changed. My academics strengthened. I found my voice in class. I made friends and began to have fun in clubs and sports. Going home at breaks began to feel odd; returning to school turned into "going home". My grades improved, as did my poise and gravitas. I was just getting going when matriculation came, too late to truly succeed at school, especially compared to my accomplished classmates. Impatient for the future, I shot out to college so fast I could have had a comet named after me. My prep school days, I thought, were history.

How wrong I was. At university and after, I began to understand how my preparatory education had changed me. My writing and oral argument had become coherent and clear. A willingness to seize opportunities and an indifference to hardships seemed second nature. As time went on I realized what I had absorbed from boarding school: self reliance; an ability to confront challenging situations and material and a growing love for such encounters; and an ease with people of varied backgrounds combined with an appreciation for traditional values and aesthetics. Without my knowledge (or consent) I had been prepped in ways far more substantive than mere college academics. I had been transformed. To misquote Nelson W. Aldrich, Jr., I left my school, but the school did not leave me.

After college came career. This included years of teaching at the university level, with admissions committee service, which brought me back in contact with the prep world. Research for various writing projects led me into prep school history and current administrative practices.

I taught at some of the schools as a visiting instructor and re-established my ties with my own as an alumni and admissions volunteer. When my own children came up to apply to schools, I had additional opportunities to closely track the school search and admission processes from an inside position. So, too, my role as a current boarding school parent and subsequent conversations with parents and professionals at an array of schools have greatly assisted my access to ongoing trends and challenges and new developments in the prep school world. As a consequence, I have learned a great deal from multiple perspectives about how boarding schools work and how to "do school well". With this knowledge has come some regret: if I had only known way back when what I know now! I had the basic sense to value my experience in my student days, but had I had access to some practical advice, I strongly suspect that my experience would have been richer and fuller.

Meanwhile, friends began to seek advice regarding the boarding school world. I offered some suggestions; more questions followed. Much of what they were asking seemed quite basic, but when I suggested that they do as I typically do, which is to research a subject in depth, they told me that there were very few books or articles available. They kept asking the same questions: "What is boarding school really like for the student? For the parents and family? What are some techniques to help a boarding student succeed?"

These are reasonable and important questions, ones to which I wish I had had the answers when I pulled my footlocker out of the family station wagon on that first rainy autumn day so long ago.

The choice to attend boarding school is a major life decision. Each applicant and applicant family would be well advised to know as much as possible about what they are getting into before they begin the arduous tasks of school searches and applications.

In hopes of helping my friends, I set about to find appropriate materials I could recommend. After some rummaging, I came to the conclusion that my friends were essentially correct. Some excellent sociological texts are decades old and increasingly obsolete. Internet sites and on-line discussions offer information haphazardly and oftentimes incorrectly. Most of the few books in print go no further than the admissions phase, the "Getting In" part of the process. "Getting In" is very important up until the student is offered admission, after which suddenly it doesn't matter at all. What does matter is "Doing School Well", a subject of much more importance in the long run and the very one that most books, in print or out, ignore. Also and not incidentally, none offered an overview of the entire experience from the family's viewpoint. This led me to the decision to write *American Prep*.

As we shall later examine in detail, boarding school is not merely a form of education. It is also a distinct culture with underlying principles and expectations. In varying degrees, prep schools retain the Old Education, education based on the liberal arts, dedicated to instilling virtue, strengthening character, and leading the student forth to discover – or begin to discover - her/his true self. Success in admissions and the quality of the campus experience depends in part on understanding this culture, its underlying values and expectations.

To begin, we must make certain reasonable assumptions. You picked up this book because, for whatever reason, you have some interest in learning more about American prep schools, boarding schools in particular. You are most likely a parent or a student; what's motivating you is a desire for a better education– with enriched academics, enhanced social contacts, an opportunity for personal growth, and superior preparation for college admission. Most likely you and your family want practical information - how do we find the "right" school and what is necessary to gain admission?

And then after, how to make the most of a boarding school education? *American Prep* is a guided tour through this entire journey, derived from personal experience and from the close observations of many others in the boarding world. It provides insights about prep culture and about how to handle the challenges that arise while at school. In these pages are tips and suggestions on subjects profound and mundane, practical and strategic. *American Prep* includes another core aspect – the emotional landscape that your journey will likely traverse.

This path is not completely linear; some aspects arise at early stages, then re-appear later. This book therefore contains deliberate repetition of some information and some circling back. There is a certain elegance to this – the boarding school world has much to do with circles and ovals, as you will soon discover. If you find that this book assists your family's journey, I shall consider it a success.

Ronald Mangravite

IT'S ALL PREP

American Prep can be of value to the student and the family whether or not the student applies to a boarding school, gains admission or graduates.

Much of the information herein can be applied to private day school issues and nearly every aspect, from first thoughts about applying on through life at boarding school, is preparation for college and adult life. That's why they call it "prep school!"

(As an added plus to students, there are plenty of SSAT vocabulary words sprinkled throughout this book!)

PART I

IS BOARDING SCHOOL FOR US?

The decision to pursue a boarding school education impacts an entire family. Because everyone needs to understand the benefits and potential drawbacks, Part I is written for all potential stake holders – the student, the parent, and other family members.

CHAPTER 1
BOARDING SCHOOL BASICS

American boarding schools are a centuries-old tradition. Many graduates have gone on to be leaders – of their nations, of business and industry, in the arts and sciences, sports, and academia. Yet, despite this distinguished history, American boarding schools remain a mystery to most people, including many families seeking a better education for their children.

The roster of American boarding schools is so vast and varied as to be bewildering to newcomers. Many are hundreds of years old with unique histories and traditions. The range of educational offerings is wide, from elite academics to specialized and remedial programs. So too is the range of opportunities, from accelerated academics and intense athletics to advanced extracurricular offerings and semester abroad programs. Some schools provide close mentoring; others foster independence. Some schools welcome a wide range of students; some are so selective, they rival Harvard's admission rates. Most offer generous financial aid to qualified families, and some of these have endowments larger than many colleges.

WHAT IS A "PREP SCHOOL"?

For most of American history, a "prep school" signified a boarding preparatory school; a non boarding preparatory school was a "private school." To be "at school" or "at prep school", meant living away from home at a boarding school.

In recent decades, the term "prep school" has lost the precise meaning it once had and now is generally but not universally used to denote all college preparatory schools, boarding and non boarding. This author much prefers the traditional terms, "prep" and private", but defers to the contemporary usage.

TYPES OF SCHOOLS

In general, American schools can be classified by two fundamental distinctions: publicly funded vs privately funded and boarding vs non boarding. This results in four separate categories: private boarding, private non boarding, public boarding, and public non boarding.

Boarding schools are private residential high schools under faculty supervision 24 hours a day. Boarding schools are self funded, through tuition and contributions from alumni and parents. They are distinguished by enhanced academics, facilities, resources, and financial resources. **Junior boarding schools**, are for younger students, some beginning at 3rd grade, some going as far as 9th grade. Some of these are stand-alone schools, others are attached to high school level boarding schools.

Private non boarding schools (known as **Day** schools) are self funded through tuition and contributions from alumni and parents. Students live at home under the supervision of their parents/guardians. Like boarding schools, day schools are typically college preparatory programs, so they are "prep schools" in the wider sense of the term.

A Day school provides education with faculty supervision during certain hours of the work week. Day school rules and culture extend into the student's off campus life, but only in a limited way: homework, sports, and perhaps extracurricular activities in the afternoons after classes and sometimes on weekends. The student otherwise escapes the school culture and its expectations.

Day schools tend to have less student diversity than boarding schools or colleges. This is due to several factors. Day schools are composed by definition of local students, lacking the geographic and international diversity of college and boarding school student enrollment. Day school tuition is expensive relative to typical American family incomes, but because of smaller endowments, day school financial aid is very limited relative to boarding schools or colleges, and usually reserved for a small number of students from underrepresented minority groups (URMs).

As a consequence, day school populations are more homogenous, from a narrow demographic of upper income and upper middle income families.

Public schools are publicly funded day schools. They are the largest group in terms of both numbers of schools and students. Funded by taxes, with close government oversight at the county, state and (increasingly) federal levels, public schools are inclusive, with a mandate to provide equal education and academic opportunities for all. Public schools are externally controlled – course content, budgets, employment, and planning are handled and/or influenced by an array of larger entities – school district administrators, state legislators, unions, and Federal guidelines – and subject to the vagaries of local, state, and national political trends. As is well known and reported, publics range widely in quality from excellent to substandard.

A hybrid subset of public schools are **charter schools**, which are privately administered but use public funds and require no tuition. Charter schools are subject to public school district curricula requirements but maintain more independence than public schools.

Public boarding schools are very rare in the United States; they number less than thirty in all, supported by state funding, offering tuition-free boarding education to in-state residents. Eligibility requirements and costs vary from school to school and state to state.

In general, in-state residency is required for tax supported tuition. Room and board is typically an extra cost, but scholarships can provide funding for such costs. Admissions are typically very competitive and focused on the student's academic record and emotional maturity. Some schools use a lottery system for applicants. In the main, public boarding schools differ from their private counterparts in two aspects – less resources and a less diverse student body. Because they are so few in number, public boarding schools will not be discussed as a group in this book. Families considering a public boarding option are advised to track many common issues in this book and contact the public boarding schools directly through TABS: The Association of Boarding Schools. See "Resources" in the Appendix.

COMPARATIVE STATISTICS

Percent of students who report that their school is academically challenging:

Boarding 91%   Day 70%   Public 50%

Percent of graduates who report being very well prepared for university academics:

Boarding 87%   Day 71%   Public 39%

Percent of graduates who report being very well prepared for university non-academic life:

Boarding 78%   Day 36%   Public 23%

Percent of students who say their schools provide leadership opportunities:

Boarding 77%   Day 60%   Public 52%

Percent of students who report being motivated by their peers:

Boarding 75%   Day 71%   Public 49%

Percent of graduates who achieve top management positions by mid-career:

Boarding 44%   Day 33%   Public 27%

Hours per week spent on homework:

Boarding 17hrs   Day 9hrs   Public 8hrs

Hours per week spent watching TV:
(a pattern that continues throughout life)

Boarding 3hrs   Day 7hrs   Public 7hrs

(source: TABS/Art & Science Group, 2003)

PERCEPTIONS AND MISPERCEPTIONS

Over its history, the boarding school world has had a disproportionate presence in popular culture. *Tom Brown's School Days*, an 1856 novel set at England's Rugby School, was wildly popular in the mid to late 19th century and has been credited for initiating American interest in English style schools. Owen Johnson's boarding school novellas, now known collectively as *The Lawrenceville Stories,* and a collegiate sequel, *Stover at Yale*, further intrigued the reading public in the early twentieth century. Later novels included James Hilton's *Goodbye, Mr. Chips* and John Knowles' *A Separate Peace*. Roald Dahl brought a contrarian view with *Boy*, a series of stories about his unhappy days at British boarding schools. Hollywood has brought the boarding world to the general public with a string of films. The *Harry Potter* films, based on the novels of J. K. Rowling, are the best known boarding school stories of all time, with worldwide distribution in scores of languages.

The modern fascination with celebrity is another source of information about boarding schools which are known for their alumni, many of whom have gone on to fame as politicians, movie stars, and titans of business. News media also bring public awareness, often of a negative sort, since they tend to report on boarding schools on occasions when bad news occurs.

This aggregate cultural history has given rise to a number of myths, often contradictory:

"Boarding schools are only for rich kids."

Due to their very high tuitions, boarding schools enroll numerous full pay students from wealthy families. Nevertheless, these schools include students of all economic backgrounds due to the schools' huge amounts of financial aid. Many schools have over 70% of their students on financial aid. Some are "need blind" and provide significant financial aid, sometimes including 100% tuition plus funding for computers, books, and travel, to families who demonstrate need. This largesse supports tuition grants to students across the economic spectrum, including students from middle class families who often qualify for much more financial aid at boarding schools than they can get from universities.

"Boarding schools are only for delinquents and troublemakers."

Some boarding schools focus on teens with major emotional and psychological issues. The "therapeutic" schools are only one category of boarding school; the large majority are college preparatory schools with a wide variety of specialties, including single sex schools, coed schools, schools focused on learning challenges, church schools, military schools, and equestrian schools. The list is long.

"Boarding schools are not diverse and exclude minorities."

This was certainly true in the two hundred and fifty year past history of American prep schools, but now the trend is strongly in the opposite direction. Enrollment of students of color reaches 40-45% in many schools. Schools also promote instructional programs in diversity, hold on-campus religious services from many faiths, and promote social tolerance.

"All boarding schools are harsh, cold, and cruel, like a Dickens novel."

Many nineteenth century American boarding schools sought to model themselves after British schools, where hazing, bullying, and corporal punishment were accepted customs until only recently. A current community of British ex-boarding school students, Boarding School Survivors, claiming permanent emotional and psychological damage from their school experiences, campaigns against British boarding schools and boarding schools in general, tarring all with the brush of their own experience.

Modern American boarding schools are a far cry from the antique British model, or indeed from what American schools once were. Today, student well-being is a top priority, with professional support from advisors, tutors, trainers, and health, dietary, psychological, and time management specialists. With extensive recreational and sports facilities, executive chefs for the dining halls, and school organic farms raising meat, dairy and produce for the dining halls, many schools are so fully equipped they are described as "country clubs with classrooms".

"You have to be an A+ student to attend boarding schools."

Another falsehood – the wide range of schools and academic programs means there's a place for every student who seeks a boarding experience, regardless of classroom success.

"A boarding school education is a sure fire route to getting into Ivy League colleges"

At one time in the 19th and 20th centuries, there was correlative data that would support this false conclusion, as certain boarding schools served as "feeder schools" to elite colleges and universities. The truth was that the admission rates from certain schools and elite colleges had much more to do with family connections than it did with the schools themselves. Now that diversity is the watchword for college admissions officers, boarding school success in college admissions, though stronger on a percentage basis than any other school category, is much lower than in decades past. Mere attendance at a boarding school is no guarantee of admission to elite colleges, nor, in truth, was it ever so.

"Boarding schools are degenerate cesspools of drugs and sexual abuse."

This canard is fostered by the media's dictum that the only news is bad news; boarding schools and prep schools in general rarely appear in the news unless something negative happens. News of misbehavior and criminal activity, especially sexual abuse, is widely reported. Despite this, statistics indicate that misbehavior at these schools is neither frequent nor widespread.

"Boarding schools are hopelessly archaic and out of step with today's world."

Historically, the leading boarding schools have been and are still at the cutting edge of modern educational techniques; they participated in the creation of Advanced Placement and SAT tests and the conference style of teaching, also known as the Harkness Method. Prep schools in general and boarding schools in particular have been quick to adopt proven pedagogical and technological advances.

A BRIEF HISTORY OF AMERICAN BOARDING SCHOOLS

The development of American boarding schools centers on two fundamental questions: how to prepare the next generation of American leadership, and from where should those young leaders come? In tandem with this ongoing concern is a through line of cultural assumptions and expectations that stretches back to the earliest days of American boarding schools and continues on to this day.

Early Days - 1760s – 1840s

In colonial times, the education of the young was a matter exclusively for the highest classes. Tutors were employed to teach both boys and girls to read and write. Formal education, which consisted of Greek, Latin, rhetoric, logic, and mathematics, was given to the boys, or at minimum the eldest boy of a family. Girls' education combined academics with social skills and the arts.

Only a handful of boarding schools, known as "academies" operated in colonial times. The term "academy" harkens back to ancient Greece and Plato's original school and has had very different meanings in different eras and cultures. In early America, an academy was understood to mean private tuition boarding secondary schools situated in towns or cities or immediately bordering them; they were not isolated or secluded. Virtually all were single sex, primarily boys' schools, though schools for girls also arose. Students boarded in private homes; gradually schools began to provide dormitory housing. Maryland's West Nottingham Academy was founded in 1744; Linden Hall, a school for girls in Pennsylvania, was founded in 1746; the Governor's Academy in Massachusetts, was founded in 1763, and North Carolina's Salem Academy, also a girl's school, began in 1772. All four flourish today. Other academies followed in the Revolutionary and post Revolutionary eras – Phillips Academy (Andover, MA), Phillips Exeter (NH), Deerfield (MA), Fryeburg (ME), Washington (ME), Cheshire (CT), Blair (NJ), Lawrence (MA), Milton (MA), Suffield (CT), Lincoln (ME) and Western Reserve (OH).

The academies promoted – and continue to promote – ideals of academic excellence, civic idealism, and social inclusivity. Andover's first African American student, Richard T. Greener, class of 1865, was also Harvard College's first black graduate. The Maidenhead Academy, later reorganized as the Lawrenceville School (NJ), enrolled students from Cuba and the Cherokee Nation as early as the 1830s. Catholic boarding schools in the United States began with the founding of the Georgetown Preparatory School (MD) in 1789. This era also saw the rise of girls' schools, including the Emma Willard School (NY) in 1814, and Miss Porter's School (CT) in 1843. Initially, the girls' schools featured social graces and less rigorous academics, but the advent of women's colleges turned the girls' schools' focus to college preparation. Military boarding schools also began in this period with Carson Long Military Academy (PA) in 1837. Virginia's Episcopal High School, the state's first high school, was founded in 1839.

The Classic Era (1850s -1950s)

The classic era of American boarding schools began with the founding of such schools as the Gunnery (CT) in 1850, the Hill School (PA) in1851, and St. Paul's School (NH) in 1856. The post Civil War era ushered in another phase of industrial expansion and massive wealth accumulation by industrialists. The families of numerous entrepreneurs suddenly became the New Rich, who sought to emulate the lifestyles of the British aristocracy. This led to the founding of several schools modeled after the classic British "public schools" - Eton, Harrow, and Rugby. Many new American boarding schools were up and running by 1899, including many of the famed schools of today – Tabor Academy (MA), Groton School (MA), Westminster School (CT), Saint George's School (RI), Saint Mark's School (MA), Thacher School (CA), Choate School (CT), Taft School (CT), Hotchkiss School (CT), Pomfret School (CT), Woodberry Forest School (VA) – sixty two in all. The next decade saw the founding of Berkshire School (MA), Cate School (CA), Kent School (CT), Mercersburg Academy (PA), Middlesex School (MA), and Trinity-Pawling School (NY), along with many others nationwide.

The schools of this era were characterized by single sex enrollment, secluded gated campuses apart from an urban center, a Protestant religious affiliation (usually Episcopalian), elite admissions which focused on upper class white Anglo Saxon Protestants (WASPs), an emphasis on British sports and British terms (e.g., using the term "forms" instead of "grades'), and the promotion of "character building". Daily chapel meetings and weekly full church services were mandatory.

The great landscape architect Frederick Law Olmstead, an Andover graduate, designed several classic prep school campuses during this era, all defined by their central circles around which the student houses/dorms and academic building were grouped. The circles gave a central focus to the community as a place for meeting, for study and for sport.

The intent of these schools was elitist – to educate the sons of the WASP upper class. They were also exclusionary, in some cases incidentally, in others by design – denying or strictly limiting admission to other groups, including Jews, Catholics, Asians, blacks, and other groups. The schools emphasized rigor and physical and mental toughness, with spare dorms, strict rules, and little free time. Sports were considered mock battle, a prelude to military service, another nod to the ideology of the British schools (Arthur Wellesley, the 1st Duke of Wellington, purportedly remarked that "the battle of Waterloo was won on the playing fields of Eton"). At the boys' schools, conflict – in the form of competition for student leadership positions, team rivalries, informal contests, and roughhousing in the dorms – was encouraged. Their cultures insisted on personal sacrifice for and submission to the group: the team, the dorm, the school.

Boarding school academics readied students for college study at a socially acceptable college: girls to the "seven sisters" – Barnard, Bryn Mawr, Mount Holyoke, Radcliffe, Smith, Vassar, and Wellesley; boys to Harvard, Yale, Amherst, Brown, Dartmouth, Williams, Swarthmore, Bowdoin, Princeton, Haverford, Middlebury, and others (the Ivy League, founded as an athletic conference in 1954, was not a point of obsession as it is now).

The elite families had long established histories with "their" colleges, and admission of their children was a foregone conclusion. The schools' prime objective was to shape up the children of the elite to make sure they could handle college academics. Several were "feeder schools" for specific colleges. In 1900, Exeter was Harvard's leading feeder school and Groton sent 19 to Harvard out of a graduating class of 23 (including Franklin Roosevelt). Between 1906 and 1932, Harvard accepted 405 Grotonians, rejecting a total of 3. Choate, Andover, and Hotchkiss regularly sent their students to Yale. Deerfield supplied Dartmouth, Williams, and Amherst. The Mercersburg class of 1928 sent 54 of its 104 graduating seniors to Princeton, (including actor Jimmy Stewart). In 1934, Hill and Lawrenceville sent more students to Princeton than all US public high schools put together.

The early 1900s saw the founding of more traditional schools as well as "progressive" schools such as Putney (VT) and Buxton (MA), which turned away from the British model with coeducation, a focus on science and nature, and inclusive admissions policies. This era also saw the rise of several prominent Catholic boarding schools like Portsmouth Abbey (RI) and Canterbury (CT).

Boarding schools of this era were the source of several pedagogical innovations, notably the Harkness or Conference Method of teaching. Begun at Exeter by its famed principal Lewis Perry with funds provided by industrialist/philanthropist Edward Harkness, the Harkness Method used a large oval wooden table for classes that emphasized discussion and connection between the students rather than lecture from the teacher. Like the campus circle, the oval Harkness table emphasized community involvement and communication. This innovation soon spread to peer schools and then throughout the prep world, where it continues on strongly today.

The Modern Era (1950s-2000)

The aftermath of World War II heralded a series of major societal and economic changes to America in general and the prep school world in particular. The economic boom of the 1950s and 60s rocketed the American middle class into prosperity. Increasing numbers of middle class students applied for college admissions; many went on to professional and business careers in numbers never seen before.

This aspirational stampede prompted universities to chart a new course for their enrollment. Instead of focusing on the children of established upper class families, college admission offices widened their focus to include the high achieving children of the middle class, whose abilities and hard work appeared to point to a new class of achievers.

Concurrent with this new opportunity for middle class students, formerly excluded groups were admitted to colleges in increasing numbers as the emerging civil rights movement in the 1950s and 60s put the issue of improved opportunities for African American students and other minority students at the forefront of social discussion.

Black students were tentatively admitted to boarding schools in the mid century. Gradually diversity became the watchword. Widespread coeducation followed soon after. Some boys and girls schools merged – Choate and Rosemary Hall, Northfield and Mount Hermon (MA), Loomis and Chaffee (CT). Most of the boys' schools added girls. The newly coed schools experienced a relaxation of the old conflict based boys' culture, more focus on the individual, and more attention to student comforts. Meanwhile, several girls' schools chose to remain single sex and have thrived, including Madeira (VA), Westover (CT), Hockaday (TX) and Dana Hall (MA).

Religion at many boarding schools also changed. Many schools dropped their religious affiliations; others watered down their religious aspects. Daily chapel morphed from a focus on prayer and sermons to school meetings, or was terminated altogether. Ecumenicalism – an acceptance and promotion of a wide array of world religions – sprang forth, with campus-based or affiliated chaplains of many faiths. Religious instruction turned from tenets of doctrine to courses in cultural history. Nevertheless, many schools have maintained their traditional church affiliations.

International students have been a presence on American boarding school campuses since the earliest days. Today, internationals are enrolling in larger numbers, bringing a global perspective to the prep school tradition, but also raising the prospect of institutional transformation. This new question of how the schools can accommodate a global population without losing their distinct cultural identities continues as a major challenge. Going forward, American boarding schools must find ways to reconcile their traditions with the forward momentum of the modern world.

OLD MONEY, NEW MONEY, AND NO MONEY

The history of boarding schools also embodies another American theme, one that has been constant through time - the establishment of elites, the rise of social mobility, and the quest for acceptance by excluded groups. The relationship between three aspects of American society – Old Money, New Money and for want of a better term, No Money, continues to play out on boarding school campuses.

Old Money derives from the earliest American elites, wealthy colonial families who devised behaviors and legal structures to ensure the preservation of capital and the means to pass it on within families from generation to generation. These families provided the wherewithal to found cultural and educational institutions, including the academies, as well as political leadership. Old Money families inherit and manage their wealth; work is not a means to acquire more money, it is an opportunity for service or personal enrichment. Since the earliest wealth in the United States derived from the British colonies and then the states created from them, the original Old Money people were and continue to be primarily WASPs.

WASP, an acronym for "White Anglo-Saxon Protestant" was first coined by the influential sociologist E. Digby Baltzell (1915-1996), himself a WASP with an elite education (St. Paul's, Penn and Columbia). Baltzell's contention that an ongoing American aristocracy was necessary to provide national leadership was tempered by his view that rising individuals from other backgrounds should join the elite based on their merits. Baltzell, who wrote from the 1950s to the 1990s, maintains influence today.

The earliest Old Money included the "Mayflower families" – the colonial New England merchants and the Dutch families who controlled New York back when it was the Dutch colony of New Amsterdam. Recently wealthy businessmen with no social background, such as John Jacob Astor, were never fully accepted, shunned as "New Money" arrivistes; in time their descendents became Old Money as well.

The rush of wealth created after the Civil War brought an entirely new wave of successful New Money families, flush with cash but lacking social credentials. These newcomers, were despised as crass, status obsessed materialists by the Old Money crowd (some of whom, of course, were rather recently considered New Money). Newly prosperous New Money families, intent on social success, were largely responsible for the sudden explosion of prep school foundings in the 1880s and 90s, the Gilded Age. These Gilded Age New Money families wanted their children to mingle with and marry into Old Money, and much of the social anxieties of the era have to do with these tensions; the novels of Henry James and Edna Ferber all do. These tensions exist in the modern era; Nelson Aldrich, Jr.'s *Old Money* (1988) limns this world in elegant detail.

According to Baltzell and Aldrich, New Money people are economically ascendant, focused on success, power, prestige, and status possessions. Trophy marriages are New Money habits. New Money relies less on extended families and more on nuclear families, yet with a focus on acquisitiveness and febrile upward striving – more money, more power, more fame, and more social acceptance. Old Money people live quietly. New Money people live large, with lavish lifestyles, leveraged assets, and public personalities. While Old Money remains mostly WASPs, New Money now includes families from every background in the world. The 20th century story of the Kennedy family and the current ones of the Trumps and the Clintons are New Money sagas of financial and political success followed by quests for social acceptance, with mixed results. New Money families seek status and prestige. Old Money families, such as the Bushes and the Roosevelts, seek to maintain relevance in a changing world.

Families without capital or social influence (let's call them No Money) didn't figure into this mix. With the exception of some scholarship students at the old academies, No Money students were not admitted to the boarding schools, nor had the means to pay the tuition even if they were accepted. This changed in the modern era with the advent of diversity and inclusion on boarding campuses. Schools which had built large endowments earmarked funds for grants for students needing tuition support. As a result, present day boarding schools include student populations from Old Money, New Money, and No Money backgrounds. This history has significance in several ways. First, boarding school is a rare circumstance in modern society where young people of radically different backgrounds mingle, work, eat, study, and socialize together on a day to day basis. One result of this is a tendency for boarding school graduates to have more understanding of "other people" than peers from their own social background may do. Another is a certain ease of communication with all sorts of people, as a consequence of this mingling.

Boarding school populations now are economically, racially, and ethnically diverse, but staffing remains remarkably traditional, with most administrators coming from the same cohort that used to populate the traditional student enrollment. Old Prep values which derived from the original Old Money values continue on: valuing service and sacrifice over individuality, and caution and comportment over free expression and exuberance. A good portion of this preference may stem from common sense – keeping a lid on a campus full of teenagers is no small task – but the underlying assumptions of restraint, service to the group, an appreciation of conformity and a suspicion of individuality appear to be due more to cultural assumptions than to pure necessity.

A FAMILY TRADITION

Some boarding schools were founded by members of the same family. The Phillips family of Massachusetts established the Phillips Academy in Andover, MA; a few years later, Phillips Exeter Academy was founded in New Hampshire. The Webb family founded not one but two Webb Schools in Tennessee, and also the Webb Schools of California. St. George's an Episcopal School, and Portsmouth Abbey, a Catholic school, were both founded by the same person, the Rev. John B. Diman.

SO WHAT IS A "PREPPY" ANYWAY?

Just as the definition of "prep school" is imprecise, so the term "preppy" (or "preppie") means different things to different people. This has some relevance to the purpose of this book.

In the beginning, a preppy was simply a young lad from an Old Money background who attended the family's boarding school as a matter of course before going on to the family's college.

The post-WWII era brought the rarified and secluded world of WASP privilege to more general attention. The "Ivy League", a termed dating from the 1930s, became firmly entrenched in American parlance when the Ivy League athletic conference was founded in 1954. Ivy League men's clothing became fashionable. Tracking this development, prep schools gained wider attention and interest. Some point to the film *Love Story* as the first wide spread use of the term "preppy", used in a somewhat mocking and negative tone, indicating a person from an upper class WASP background and their manner of dress and behavior.

In 1980, a book was published that changed that definition – probably by accident. *The Official Preppy Handbook*, a witty insouciant satire on prep culture, became an instant best seller and a "how-to" handbook for determined status seekers. The result was a shift in the meaning of "preppy" from an underlying WASP lifestyle (and its fundamental values) to a fashion trend: "preppy style". This expanded into a lifestyle choice one could acquire. A prep school education became a status symbol to collect, along with other preppy accoutrements – Volvo station wagons, pure bred dogs, and summer vacations in certain acceptable zip codes.

The prep craze was magnified by intense marketing. Ralph Lauren, who began his career with Ivy/prep mainstay Brooks Brothers, recognized this marketing opportunity and has exploited it ever since. Popular Merchandise, Inc, aiming for a Ralph Lauren look at a much lower price point, rebranded itself as J. Crew, a fabricated name referencing the ultimate Ivy clothier J. Press and the uber-prep sport, crew.

The prep style continues as it always has, waxing and waning in popularity. The damage, however, has been done. The whimsical sprezzatura of the earlier Old Money era carries on, but it has been nearly overwhelmed by a relentless, rather desperate New Money search for status. With the latter comes a grim focus on all prep schools, boarding and day, as commodities, status markers, and stepping stones to the next aspirational plateau: elite college placement. As a result, the term "preppy" now signifies a shallow materialism, ostentation, and self aggrandizement, values quite at odds with its origins.

WHEN IS PREP NOT PREP?

The terminology in this book is specifically American. British and Commonwealth schools use similar terms but for entirely different meanings:

AMERICAN USAGE	BRITISH USAGE
High School	College
University or college	University
Junior boarding school (pre high school)	Prep school
Prep School or Boarding School (high school)	Public school
Government chartered high school	Academy

Additionally, American usage makes a distinction between boarding "schools" and "academies".

And as noted, to muddy things further, the American usage of "prep school" can mean either a preparatory boarding school or preparatory schools in general, whether boarding or non boarding.

CHAPTER 2
BOARDING SCHOOLS TODAY

Modern American boarding schools strive to balance their enduring community traditions with a forward thinking stance towards educational innovation and societal change. Academics are supported by co-curricular and experiential learning after class, day and night, in sports and activities, at meals, in the dorms, with frequent extra class contact with teachers who also coach sports and oversee dorm life. Teachers and students also interact at meals and at social events — coffees and teas, school rallies and other events, all additional opportunites for discussion and learning. The Schools are in essence a collegiate environment but with close adult supervison.

Boarding schools are highly social and self contained; students rarely leave the campus community. A widely diverse student body is norm, with students from different ethnic, racial, geographic, income, and national backgrounds. Minority representation is much higher than at private day schools.

Financial aid tends to be much more ample and available than at day schools. As a consequence, these schools enroll large numbers of students from middle and lower income backgrounds. Also, families with incomes too high to qualify for financial aid at day schools often find that they are eligible for aid at boarding schools.

Issues of status and prestige are deliberately controlled. All boarders live in dorm rooms which are typically spare and small. This uniformity and lack of space diminishes status of possessions. Instead, school policies enchance the status of rank (upperclassmen over underclassmen) and success (through positions of leadership in academics, athletics and activies).

Today's boarding school typically provide advanced systems for student support — counseling, advising, tutoring, medical and psychological care, sports training and therapy with fully equipped facilities and resources in support of these services. Certain school policies enhance student safety. Campuses have 24 hour security.

Drugs and alcohol are banned, and while such bans are not 100% effective, student access to these substances is more restricted than at day and public schools. Boarding students typically do not have cars at school, nor are they allowed to ride in cars without express parental permission. Off campus trips are controlled and require faculty permission.

Challenges remain. Elitism is an ongoing concern. The schools continue to strive for excellence and to prepare young students – now coming from every cultural and societal background – to assume the mantle of leadership in the society of the future. How this equates with the schools' professed values of democracy, equality, and social justice remains an unresolved question.

Blacks and Hispanics continue to be underrepresented in prep student populations, as are students from lower income families. Many schools have responded with vigorous financial aid support, including some programs offering free tuition to families under certain annual income levels.

The status of LGBT students remains a subject of controversy as school attempts to promote tolerance and support for these students comes into conflict with traditionally minded alumni.

The intense pressures of boarding school life have prompted some schools to step down some of their programming to allow students more free time. Recent sex assault scandals and revelations of others from decades past have resulted in new prevention and reporting policies on many campuses. Boarding students' success in elite college admissions has fallen significantly compared to rates in decades past, but continue to strongly outperform compared to day schools and public schools.

THE ADMINISTRATIVE STRUCTURE OF BOARDING SCHOOLS

Trustees are the legal owners of the school; organized as a corporate board of directors, trustees are volunteers chosen for their sagacity and business acumen. Trustees tend to be very successful players in the business or professional communities. They are often alumni/ae, sometimes parents, or occasionally outsiders who are major donors. One of the trustees' most critical functions is to choose the Head of school; a poor choice can affect the school for years after. Their second function is to consider and approve or deny major proposals such as new construction programs as well as tuition raises or reductions. Their third main role is to assist the Head to manage any major crisis that may arise. Trustees typically travel twice a year to the campus for general meetings, take on committee work, and spend many more volunteer hours in other school service. Trustees usually are very slow to interfere with the school's normal operations, but their gravitas and legal power can be brought to bear in times of challenge or crisis.

Heads of School go by various titles – Principal, Rector, Director, Headmaster, Head Master or simply Head. The Head is the spokesperson of the school and articulates its fundamental principles and a vision for the future. The Head also embodies the school and serves as chief executive of the school's business organization, which is quite often a multi-million dollar entity. The position also requires a great deal of political and social intelligence. The great school Heads have somehow managed to balance all these demands, but typically Heads tend to be stronger in some areas than in others.

Heads who are weak in finances can steer their ship onto the reefs, while corporate types can fail to sufficiently cater to the various constituencies in the school communities. The impact of a new Head takes a while to take effect and lasts well after departure.

Administrators serve at the pleasure of the Head. Each department – Facilities, Development, Alumni Relations, and so forth – is charged with implementing the policies set by the Head and the Trustee. Sometimes a school's power structure tips the other way, with a Head articulating policies generated by the departments.

The administrators of most concern to applicants and their parents include the **Dean or Director of Admission,** who is charged with putting together the incoming class (usually 9th grade, though a few schools begin at 8th grade) as well as adding new members to upper classes to replace those who withdraw or are expelled. The Dean of Admission is the face of the school for applicants, manages a staff of assistant and associate directors, and oversees the very central task of meeting the enrollment needs of the school. Admission is a personnel management field that must balance an array of constituencies and needs, including the school's need for certain student assets – academics, athletics, arts, and diversity are prominent examples.

Admission departments increasingly use data management and forecast modeling to put together strong classes of incoming students. The arrival of a skilled and gifted Dean of Admission can have an immediate impact on a school community; so too, it must be noted, can the departure of one. The **Director of Financial Aid** manages decisions about which admitted students will receive financial aid, under what terms and conditions, and in what amounts. As with some colleges, some prep schools are adding a **Dean or Director of**

Enrollment Management. This senior officer manages enrollment after the admission process, including such issues as attrition (why students withdraw from the school) and yield (why students chose one school over others). Information drawn from these inquiries has tremendous promise for schools' efforts to improve their "customer appeal". There is however a potential negative consequence for applicants seeking entry in the higher grades, as fewer spaces come available due to fewer students withdrawing. The organization of these officers – who reports to whom - varies from school to school.

Faculty: Boarding school educators are unique in the American teaching community, resembling something like a cross between their private day peers and college professors. They have considerable freedom to shape their own curricula, but often receive research support from the schools for their own academic activities. An additional characteristic of boarding school faculty is that a sizable percentage are alumnae/i of the schools where they teach, adding another layer of commitment and cultural cohesion. As with teachers at private day schools, they are not unionized and usually are not formally tenured. Many agree to a multiyear commitment that includes dorm supervisory service. The partners and/or children of dorm faculty help create a family atmosphere for the students. The masters' children often grow up to attend the school, provided their academics are sufficient. Many teachers serve their entire working lives at one school; some even bequeath their estates to their schools.

Traditionally, many faculty at boys' schools were "triple threats", serving as instructors, athletic coaches and dorm supervisors. At girls' schools, academic, athletic, and residential staffs have typically been kept separate. At present, the tradition of the "triple threat" boarding school teacher is in decline.

Boarding school **alumni** have traditionally held positions of importance in the school power structure. Since boarding schools lack access to research and government grants, they are much more dependent on alumni support than are colleges and universities. This gives alumni a continued voice in school decisions. The admission prospects of alumni children, known as "legacies", are thereby more enhanced than legacies at most colleges. Alumni tend to be very active in volunteer work, serving on fund raising and admissions committees and conducting applicant interviews and other pro bono work for their schools.

Students also have a voice in the school administration, despite their youth and brief tenure on campus. Student government maintains a dialogue with the head of school and the faculty about student concerns and serves as a bridge between adult officialdom and the student body. Student prefects help maintain order in the dorms and serve as peer counselors and observers. The schools, ever mindful that many students come from families with long standing school loyalty and that all students quickly become alumni, have adopted a long term viewpoint about students; that goofy fifteen-year-old may turn into an enthusiastic billionaire donor in the blink of an eye.

Parents once were an afterthought in boarding school culture. Poor transportation reduced parental contact to rare campus visits. Parent-student communication consisted of regular correspondence and the occasional "care package". Today's enhanced travel options and high tech communications have changed all of that. Parents are increasingly active in the life of the schools. Through parents' organizations, many parents help as volunteer admissions interviewers, host regional receptions for families of applicants, assist in fund raising, and speak as school advocates. Long distance parents maintain frequent contact with their students as well as with teachers, dorm supervisors, tutors, and advisors. Streaming video services allow parents to follow sporting events and school assemblies. Local parents serve as surrogate parents for international and long distance domestic students; as volunteer activity hosts, providing snacks and drinks to sports teams; and as weekend or holiday hosts for students too far from home to travel on breaks. Many parents maintain their school ties long after their children have graduated.

THE BOARDING SCHOOL CAMPUS

Boarding school history plays out in the configuration of campuses. The old academies continue to border towns, often with public streets traversing the school grounds. The English style schools from the late 19th century maintain gated campuses, with academic and administrative buildings and student housing grouped around lawns bordered by trees. Schools dating from the modern era are arranged in a variety of patterns, according their individual histories. The athletic facilities and playing fields tend to sit further off, though some schools maintain their athletic fields at the center of their campuses.

The typical distribution of buildings on a boarding school campus means that students get a lot of exercise hiking from one building to another. Even those schools with compact campuses require considerable walking – to classes, to sports events, or to the nearby town. As mentioned previously, cars are forbidden to boarding students at most schools; and day students, who may drive to and from school with parental and school permission, must park their car upon arrival and walk the campus like everyone else. As a result, despite a demanding study schedule, boarding school students get outdoors regularly, in every kind of weather. A school closure due to severe weather is a decided rarity – most schools soldier on through rain, wind, and snow.

HOUSING

Boarding school students are typically housed in dormitories on campus. Each has on-site adult supervision – masters and advisors – plus a system of student assistants to maintain dorm rules and lead group activities. Dorm masters are faculty, usually a master and an assistant master, sometimes multiple assistant masters, who live on site in their own apartments within the dorm. Often the assistant doubles as an academic advisor, or an advisor is attached as a nonresident. In addition, schools often have other nonresident faculty attached to the dorms who serve as supervisors when the resident master is absent. Student assistants, often known as "prefects" or "proctors", act as semiofficial supervisors, keeping order and offering guidance and advice to younger and new students. Prefects can also serve as informal confidants, as students sometimes feel more comfortable revealing secrets to other students rather than speaking to adult authority figures. Prefects are often given training on how to spot and respond to signs of student depression, emotional crisis, substance abuse, and other issues.

Most dorms are single sex, though some few schools have coed dorms, with girls on some floors and boys on others. Some schools have "vertically integrated" dorms, where students from all grade levels live together. The benefit to this is that the younger students learn from the older ones and the older students learn to mentor the younger ones. Others have dorms by grade level, with younger students grouped together, tenth and eleventh graders together, and seniors in their own residences. The benefits here are that students have different needs and interests at different ages, and the gradual lessening of school restrictions as the students mature is more easily managed when they are grouped by grade. Seniors only housing also can simulate a college experience, with no 'lights out' restrictions and other liberties.

A tiny cadre of schools opt for a **house system** based on the classic British boarding school house systems, such as at Eton and Rugby. The Lawrenceville School established a house system in 1880. Its near neighbor, the Hun School of Princeton (NJ) also has a house system, as does the Chaminade Preparatory School in St. Louis MO, the University School (non boarding) in Ohio and McCracken County High School, a public school in Kentucky. Like residential colleges at some universities (such as at Yale), boarding school houses are a subset of dorms in function, but with more group identity, history, and cohesion. Houses have their own histories, flags, colors, and traditional house rivalries. Dorms and houses both have student governments that help organize social and housekeeping events, decorate the common areas, and promote student spirit. Dorm and house government service is often a stepping stone to school wide student government positions.

Boarding school housing varies widely in size and quality but is often better than at colleges. As a rule the dorms are deliberately spare and basic. There are specific rules regarding lights out, noise levels, and quiet times. Student prefects on each floor maintain order, serve as informal counselors, and conduct room inspections. These inspections vary widely. Some schools require regular and frequent inspections, while at others inspections are an afterthought.

Space and light are always issues; usually there is little of either. The larger, brighter, quieter rooms go to ongoing students who get seniority in room selection. New students tend to be stuck with what's left over. Once in a while a lucky newbie gets a great room when a longtime returning student suddenly withdraws at the last moment.

Storage space in most dorm rooms is nearly nonexistent, except for under one's bed. Sunlight is problematic. South facing rooms sometimes get too much, north facing rooms too little. Despite the incredible array of facilities and programs at boarding schools, many, perhaps most, prep dorm rooms have no air conditioning, so dorms at schools in even the most northern of climes tend to be stiflingly hot at the start of fall term and the end of spring term.

Due to safety and sanitation concerns, schools have numerous rules about what can be kept, hung, or used in the dorms. Anything involving heat and fire – toaster ovens, coffee makers, candles, irons, and the like are prohibited. Flammable wall hangings, pets, and firearms all are no-nos. Small appliances such as refrigerators and televisions usually do not make the cut. One device that is often welcome is a vacuum cleaner (and everyone will want to borrow it!).

Boarding school dorms have specific check in/check out times. A Duty Master, usually a faculty member, is present each evening to monitor check in times. Students are expected to check in by a prescribed hour and remain in their dorms until six or seven the next morning. Students seeking to leave their dorms after check in need permission from the Duty Master. Weekend evenings usually have more relaxed rules. Permissions are also required for off campus trips and weekend overnight trips. The upper grades usually have more privileges.

'THE FOUR As'

Most schools revolve around four basic core concerns – academics, athletics, arts, and activities – **the Four A's**. Most of the schools emphasize and promote student participation in all four as aspects of a multidimensional education. This presents students with the challenge of a continual balancing act requiring the student to marshal limited reserves of time and energy to fulfill sometimes conflicting demands.

ACADEMICS

American boarding schools offer a range of academic styles and philosophies. In the main, coursework tends toward small classes, extended class discussion, and extensive individual attention from instructors. The schools cleave to the traditional liberal arts, with courses in literature, history, science, mathematics, and languages. As preparation for college, this tradition has become increasingly pertinent to a student's education as even elite colleges turn towards pre-professional programs or wide-open requirement-free curricula. In several surveys at elite universities, large majorities of boarding school alums have expressed disappointment with their college education, in comparison with what they received "at school."

The majority of the schools also feature heightened academic demands – more reading, more homework, and more expectations from essays and projects. Class participation is enhanced, routine reliance on objective testing diminished. In the most demanding of the boarding schools, these standards are extremely rigorous.

Traditionally, many boarding schools brought in new students at the eighth grade level, but now, with the exception of Groton and a few others, most school start at ninth grade. Many schools ease first year students into academics with instruction in time management, essay construction, and study techniques, pass/fail grading in the first term, and scheduled study halls and early lights out in the dorms, all overseen by residential faculty and academic advisors. After the first year, these strictures are gradually loosened as the students mature; less supervision and more work is the standard. Eventually, students near graduation will be given many more freedoms and a heavy work load so that the transition to college is smooth.

Boading schools tend to favor the Harkness or conference method, with students and teacher grouped around a large oval table. Learning is based on discussion and questioning rather than lecture and the absorption of facts. Students are expected to read widely and ahead of the discussions. Testing is infrequent. The writing of papers is central. Some few schools, including most famously Exeter, employ the conference method for every subject, including mathematics and the lab-based sciences. Others pick and choose, limiting the conference method to the humanities and languages.

For new students coming from public schools, boarding school academics can come as a shock. Those coming from private day schools will often feel comfortable with the conference teaching style, but the level of intensity tends to be higher. Those from junior boarding schools usually have a seamless transition as they are already accustomed to these conditions. New students often bloom when presented with the conference method and participate well in class. Where they tend to falter is in note taking and especially in reading. The result is often an abrupt grade drop in the first term, a startling and dismaying circumstance for new students, and one that is often a first in their lives. New students entering after the first year suffer most in this circumstance, as many schools do not give older new students the tutorial and oversight support that the youngest grade receives. In the past, boarding school grading was rigorous; achieving a B average was often a hard fought campaign. Nowadays, as is the case with their college brethren, these schools sometimes struggle with bouts of grade inflation as average scores trend upward. This is sometimes explained as a reaction to correlative grade inflation at private day and public schools. Purgative remedies at some schools sometimes result in grade deflation, with protests from students and parents.

Overall, straight A averages are a decided rarity at boarding school. Grade point averages (GPAs) are kept for each student at some schools while others dispense with this. Many schools maintain Cum Laude societies, recognizing students whose academics place them in the top 20% of their class.

Most curricula are tightly prescribed; students proceed from one term to the next and one year to the next with many required courses and few options. New students test in various subjects to place them in levels of courses – regular, honors, or advanced. The wide array of electives, often a delight to read through in the school catalogues, is usually reserved for students in their eleventh and twelfth grade years.

In class, new students tend to fall into one of two camps. Some keep quiet, too shy or intimidated to speak. For many, sitting in a classroom configuration making eye contact with the other students is a new and strange experience. Others who may be more familiar with the conference method may feel compelled to show off their intellect by discoursing at length, without regard to the opinions of others. Both extremes need to learn to engage other students, listen to alternative viewpoints, and develop nuanced responses from those interchanges.

Schools have a variety of strategies regarding course selection and loads. Eleventh grade is typically the most challenging year, with added courses and/or more rigor. New students entering a school past the lowest grade need to understand the details of that school's course structure well ahead of arrival.

Boarding school teachers and students encounter one another in many more circumstances than at non boarding schools. Student/teacher conversations happen in after class discussions, in the library, at meals and, in the common rooms in the dorms. Teachers often invite their students to coffees or teas and see them during sports practice or at other campus events.

The schools also maintain staffs of **advisors.** Academic advisors usually are faculty members and are often attached to dorms as assistant masters. Many schools employ time management and/or organizational advisors to help new students. A battery of certified psychologists, physicians, nutritionists, physical therapists, and sports trainers are common on boarding campuses. Many schools also allow students to secure outside tutors who are given permission to meet with students on campus. Advanced athletes in some sports specialties may receive permission to train with outside coaches off campus.

Students with **ADD/ADHD and learning differences** will find a widely varying range of support from school to school. All must comply with the requirements of the Americans with Disbilities Act (ADA), but some go much further, with entire school departments dedicated to such support. Such schools usually charge extra fees for students who wish to use these facilities. Some schools are completely dedicated to students with special needs.

ATHLETICS

Sports play a traditional and central role in boarding school life. Many schools have three sports requirements (fall-winter-spring) for all students. Sports help schools promote student health and fitness, divert adolescent energy away from misbehavior, and teach an array of "character building" values: sportsmanship, cooperation, team dynamics, leadership, determination, and not incidentally, resilience after failure.

The focus on sports comes as a culture shock to many new students, including public and day students whose schools have dropped physical education requirements and particularly those from other countries, where athletics are often not part of a school curriculum and not regarded as a useful student activity at all. Some schools have compromised by offering non sports activities such as yoga, dance, and rock climbing to substitute for competitive sports.

For many student athletes, a boarding school is a huge toy box of fantastic, well funded sports programs that offer an array of helmet sports – football, lacrosse, baseball, hockey – as well as track and field, crew, field hockey, equestrian, wrestling, fencing, golf, skiing and many more programs. With public high school sports increasingly reserved for those with experience and exceptional skill, boarding schools often offer students a chance to try new sports, working their way up from squads of absolute beginners known as "thirds" to junior varsity and varsity levels.

Small schools offer more chances for students to play at the varsity level. Large schools often have a wider range of sports offerings. Schools that do not field teams in a sport usually have a club for that sport or are willing to support one on student request. As larger schools tend to play sports at a higher level than the smaller schools, truly gifted athletes tend to enroll in the larger schools.

Rigorous sports activity promotes school spirit, intense camaraderie among teammates, and the potential for college athletic scholarships. Many advanced high school athletes take postgraduate (PG) years at boarding schools to continue their physical training, improve their skills, add playing time, and gain the attention of college sports scouts. This sometimes presents disappointment for student athletes who after working their way up for years towards a starting position on a team find themselves displaced by an incoming star athlete.

Boarding school sports have downsides. Injury can complicate life on a campus that requires a lot of walking and carrying. Team travel to and from rival schools can take up a lot of time. Students who repeat years, either upon entry to the school or as PGs, sometimes run afoul of college sports eligibility rules. Students in such circumstances need to work closely with school athletic departments to comply with NCAA rules.

Schools sometimes "find" their star athletes on campus. Many a lanky cross country runner (fall sport) has been invited to join a school's crew squad (spring sport), and stick handling hockey players (winter) end up playing lacrosse in the spring. Truly exceptional prep athletes competing at the Olympic and international circuit level are given leeway by schools to travel to compete or train. Some will take a year's absence to do this, returning to school afterwards.

ARTS

The arts, especially the performing arts, play a central role in boarding school communities. Theatre, music, and dance provide the campuses with entertainment and cultural enrichment critical to resident student populations who lack easy access to off campus events.

The arts are also central to school mandates for personal expression and exploration and community participation. In a number of schools, performing arts, particularly dance, can serve to satisfy athletic requirements.

Not incidentally, the arts also serve as excellent public relations tools for the schools. School choral groups, dance and theatre presentations, and orchestral and jazz/pop concerts help enliven school admission programs, revisit days, parent weekends, graduation exercises, alumni events, and assorted school celebrations. Student artists serve as goodwill ambassadors when schools invite nearby community residents to student performances and exhibitions.

The schools promote the arts with extraordinary faculty and with facilities of a quality that often surpasses those at colleges or even in some instances those found in the professional arena. Students bringing high levels of arts talent help raise the bar for others looking to explore arts fields. It is no coincidence that many well known artists and performers have prep school backgrounds.

ACTIVITIES

Extracurricular activities – clubs, community service, travel programs, and the like - are a critical aspect of campus culture. Students are expected to participate as a matter of community involvement, but there is also an aspect of self-interest, since a commitment to school publications, leadership, and public service helps students gain the attention of college admissions officers. At American prep schools, activities serve as leadership opportunities for those who serve in student government, as editors of school publications, and as officers of community outreach clubs. Specialty clubs also act as laboratories for students to explore potential career options: debate club, investment club, engineering and science clubs, etc. The range of clubs and opportunities is staggering; many schools offer well over a hundred different clubs.

STUDENT SUPPORT SYSTEMS

American boarding schools typically offer extensive support systems for their students. Advisors are available around the clock. On campus health facilities offer an array of medical services. Many schools provide educational counselors and tutors, time management and organizational specialists, as well as nutritionists, physical therapists and trainers. Psychological and emotional health support, once nonexistent on boarding campuses, is now a central concern. Staff psychologists and counselors are on call for students experiencing depression, anxiety, or other personal issues, and faculty, staff, and student assistants are trained to identify students who may need help. Many schools require assemblies and student workshops to address issues of both misbehavior and wellness.

MISBEHAVIOR

Misbehavior on a boarding school campus, especially anything of a sexual or criminal nature, can be cause for parental concern. With a resident population of teenagers, the potential for trouble is always present. However, there is no data that suggests that boarding schools experience student misbehavior at comparable or higher rates than day or public schools. The close adult supervision tends to work to suppress bad behavior, but incidents do occur. Such events bear close attention if systemic administrative failures have resulted – failure to discover ongoing problems, failure to expose them once discovered, and/or failure to appropriately punish offenders – which speak to a collapse of leadership that will likely be evident in other less critical areas of that school's life. Rules regarding misbehavior vary widely, but all schools have detailed specific procedures regarding various types of infraction as well as their severity. All is revealed in the school's student manual. Students may ignore much of their school's manual without much consequence, but understanding the school's rules about misbehavior is essential Minor infractions typically involve behavior that does not involve aggression towards others or damage of property. Such offenses are usually punished by detention, loss of privileges and other short term restrictions. Major transgressions, involving threat or harm to others, property damage, or serious ethical lapses may be met with harsher punishments – longterm restriction of privileges, probation, suspension, or dismissal.

Some schools are "one strike", meaning that the commission of one major offense is cause for expulsion. Others are "two strike" allowing a student to remain at school after a major offense, often with restrictions and on probation. The "two strike" provision does not apply to truly egregious misbehavior.

Cheating— including plagiarism – the claiming of written work by others as one's own – has become common in all sorts of high schools, as students pull down texts from the Internet. Educators now use plagiarism detection software to identify these abuses, and punishments can be severe, including expulsion. Cheating likewise is often an expellable offense.

Sexual misconduct is one area subject to much scrutiny. Some schools have specific rules of conduct to ensure sexual encounters are clearly consensual. Despite these rules, sexual misconduct does occur, though this is rare, as it is at other types of high schools. To add more uncertainty, sexual misconduct laws vary widely from state to state.

Bullying, harassment, and hazing are also serious offenses. Bullying can occur in person, online, on the phone, and in other ways. Harassment, which can include sexual harassment, and prejudicial behavior because of one's race, ethnicity, religion, gender, or sexuality can also occur in many forms and settings. Many schools have diversity officers trained in such issues who can respond to student reports of bias.

Illegal drug use is banned and alcohol use is forbidden to most students on most boarding campuses, though some schools allow alcohol to students who are legal adults under certain restricted circumstances. Schools work out their own policies for substance infractions. Some take a stern line with drugs but tend to treat alcohol much less harshly. Others are equally strict with both. Students caught selling drugs face immediate dismissal, and in the case of a serious criminal action, potential arrest. Some schools maintain sanctuary policies for students who take alcohol or drugs but then recognize their errors, self report their behavior and check into the student health center. Another common policy is nondisciplinary intervention (NDI), whereby a student or faculty member can alert a school official of a student's alcohol or drug use, or a student can self report. The school then moves to help the offending student without disciplinary action.

Responses to criminal behavior may depend on the gravity of the offense. A petty theft might land a student on probation with warnings, but not expulsion or arrest. Repeated acts of theft that reveal a student unwilling or unable to reform, or a theft of real magnitude that sullies the school's reputation may result in suspension, dismissal, or arrest.

Schools will go a long way to avoid such extreme measures. Once the school is aware of a problem, administrators will contact the parents to discuss the potential consequences. Such steps usually put a stop to the issue ahead of a major crisis. Detection of student problems is largely dependent on the web of communications systems that schools put into place. This includes faculty, advisors, student proctors, and the general population working together when someone becomes aware of serious malfeasance. Some school communities are decidedly better at this than others.

COLLEGE COUNSELING

As a rule, college advising at boarding schools is much more sophisticated than at public and day schools. Boarding school college counselors (CCs) often have long standing personal relationships with the admissions officers (AOs) of elite colleges. They often invite college AOs to campus, travel to colleges to lobby for their students, and closely advise the students about their applications.

College advising usually begins with general guidance for students in 9th and 10th grade, with admonitions to take rigorous courses in core subjects, participate in extracurricular activities (ECs) and service, and use summer vacations to good purpose. Many schools explicitly avoid college admission activities until the students reach 11th grade to keep their students focused on school, not college.

The college admission push typically kicks off in the middle of 11th grade (with some schools working with students in 10th grade). It often begins with a family weekend during the winter term. Parents and students meet in large groups with CCs, then with individual counselors assigned to small groups of students. These private sessions focus on what the students are seeking in a college (similar to the boarding school search process), and also on the extent of the family's financial resources.

CCs will use this information together with student test scores and transcripts to propose a slate of prospective colleges. Many schools use software programs such as Naviance to assist in this task. By comparing a student's test scores and transcripts against those of recent school alumni, the software programs can project likely college matches. Naviance is widely used by a wide range of high schools both public and private, but often to only limited effect if the school's statistical base is small; a "B" rated public school which has only one grad matriculated to Dartmouth, and that ten years ago, cannot accurately predict the probabilities for a current applicant from that school to that college. whereas a boarding school with multiple recent admittees would have stronger data with which to work.

College admissions officers and boarding school CCs are closely connected, communicate frequently, and often socialize together. Many pros move from one camp to the other somewhat as realtors do, representing the "buyer" (the college), and then shifting over to work for the "seller" (the school). The familiarity between these two camps often means that school CCs frequently learn breaking news that could impact their students: perhaps what positions a college sports team is looking to fill, what the appointment of a new college admissions director may bode for the school's rising applicants, or upcoming changes in financial aid calculations. CCs can also promote their star students to the colleges ahead to their applications.

The CCs have a vested interest in this process. They want to maximize their school's "admit efficiency" and therefore promote students who are strong candidates likely to gain admission to a particular college and also likely to accept a place when offered. This increases the college's admissions efficiency, ups their "yield" (admitting students who go on to enroll), and raises the college's confidence in that school's college counselors, thereby improving the chances for future applicants recommended by those CCs. This is why CCs often dissuade less than stellar students from taking "long shot" chances on colleges that will most likely reject them.

CCs also manage students' application plans against the plans of other classmates. Though the notion that elite colleges take quotas of students from certain schools is decidedly false, large numbers of students applying to the same college increases the likelihood of more rejections, if for no other reason than that colleges prefer diversity of geography and school origin. CCs cannot and do not prevent students from applying to long shot schools, but do help their students understand their likely prospects and promote realistic strategies to achieve them.

Each student is given a list of likely prospective colleges by the CCs. This is partly to help the students understand where they will likely be accepted. It also helps the CCs, as each college relies on the school's CCs to weed out the unlikely candidates from the applicants most likely to be accepted and to attend that college.

The advantages of boarding school college counseling are many. Fully staffed CC offices provide a depth and frequency of individual counseling that other schools lack. Students are given schedules to maintain – advance study for and scheduling of SAT/ACT exams and SAT subject tests. Parents are kept advised of progress. Many boarding schools host college AOs to interview students on campus. College coaches likewise are invited to observe prep athletes.
However, boarding school students face certain particular challenges in college admissions. Since prep schools by definition consist of students preparing for college, this usually results in many students applying to the same few colleges, usually those ranked in the top 20 or 30, a circumstance not so common in other types of schools, where a minority of students might be college bound (as in most public schools) or focused on local or in state colleges (as in many day schools). This results in much more potential intra-school competition

at the boarding schools. Tensions and emotions can rise. Students often respond to this by avoiding discussion of their grades, tests scores, and college plans, thereby helping to maintain a friendly atmosphere before acceptances are mailed and hurt feelings and resentments are generated. Boarding schoolers may also find themselves at a disadvantage geographically. Whereas a student at a boarding school might gain some small advantage being from an underrepresented state, the school itself might be in Connecticut, an overrepresented state. In such cases, students must make sure that their applications emphasize their family's location, not their school's.

The schools typically allow 12th grade students to take a small number of "college days" in the fall and winter to visit prospective colleges. Students travelling to far off colleges often schedule college days on a Friday or Monday to combine with the weekend days in order to accommodate long distance travel. "Revisit days" handle similar travel needs after college admission offers have been received in the spring.

MINORITIES

The experience of minorities at boarding schools continues to evolve. In a repudiation of their past history, these schools now are committed to inclusive and diverse student populations and seek to foster tolerance and empathy amongst students from differing backgrounds. Minorities still face challenges navigating issues of race, ethnicity, religion, and sexual identity within boarding communities and also with their surrounding localities, which are often not nearly so progressive in their viewpoints as are the schools themselves.

LGBT students will find a range of situations depending on the school. Many schools have strong support groups and a culture of support; others offer official tolerance but with some hostility within the student population. As these circumstances are fluid and can change quickly, it makes sense to fully investigate schools as they are at the time of application, and not to rely on information that could be several years out of date.

INTERNATIONAL STUDENTS

Internationals have a long tradition in American boarding schools. In the past, internationals were a small population, with only a few students from the same country. Now international populations are growing quickly, in enough numbers at some schools that students can speak their native languages for much of each day, speaking English primarily in class. This can be counterproductive for many international families who may be sending their children to American schools to perfect their fluency in English and for cultural immersion. Internationals also find a wide range of support at the schools, with some schools providing "host" families to serve in loco parentis for students from far away. These families maintain contact with the student's families and keep them up to date with their students' activities via Skype and social media. Other schools' cultures do not offer such levels of support for internationals.

WHO GOES TO BOARDING SCHOOLS?

Boarding school students now come from a wide array of classes, races, ethnicities, cultures and lifestyles. Despite this diversity, all students and their families have one or more basic motives for choosing a boarding school education. These include:

LEGACY TRADITION

Students whose parents and forebears attended the same school are known as legacies. Legacy families usually have a firm commitment of support for that school and regularly contribute money and volunteer hours. Because of this tradition, legacy students typically receive preferential treatment in admission, as is customary with most colleges.

In the past, legacy students were the norm at boarding schools. Nowadays, legacies are less prevalent, often a minority population. Legacies often follow in the family footsteps – the same dorms/houses, sports, courses, and even at times teachers. Their lifelong affiliation with the school often gives legacies a relaxed confidence that can have a calming effect on campus, helping to moderate the anxieties of newcomers.

ACADEMIC EXCELLENCE & POSITIVE LEARNING ENVIORNMENTS

Many students apply to boarding schools seeking superior academic opportunities and programs. Such students often are refugees from schools where academic effort is derided. The intellectually curious generally meet with social approval on boarding campuses. Advanced students are often thrilled to enter a school where the student body values and appreciates learning and hard work.

Many incoming students are gifted intellectually but, discouraged by their past school experience, have mediocre records of achievement. Such students often blossom under the tutelage of boarding school academics, with enchanced individual attention and academic support.

ESCAPING PROBLEMS AT HOME

Some students come from family situations that negatively influence study and academic progress due to parental strife, terminal or debilitating illness or other crises. A boarding school can be a haven in such instances but many a student in such situations has suffered residual after effects; a young person's transition away from familial adversity can be difficult. Fortunately, contemporary boarding schools have counseling staffs at the ready to assist in such cases.

(Note: this strategy may work if the student's problems are external; students who carry unresolved emotional or psychological issues often do not find relief at boarding school.)

CHARACTER/SOCIAL DEVELOPMENT

Families sometimes seek out boarding schools to help their students gain self-reliance, responsibility, and personal identity apart from the family. Students who come from very wealthy or celebrity backgrounds often thrive in the relative social equity of a boarding school campus. Such students may have the freedom to find their own core identity, apart from their family backgrounds.

Boarding schools, with their objective authority and systems of acceptable behavior, can allow rebellious students a neutral environment to sort through their conflicted feelings about their families and channel their emotions in constructive paths. Students from very protective households can find self reliance; those from tightly directed households can find independence; both can find self assurance. Boarding school life fosters emotional intelligence – negotiation, reconciliation, cooperation and resilience. Equally, these schools understand negative education – learning to cope with failure, defeat and disappointment.

FAMILIES IN TRANSIT

Families that move frequently because of corporate reassignment, government postings, or similar circumstances will often send their students to boarding school to give them the comfort and continuity of a home base. Students from such families often become the most connected of all students. Lacking a home circle of friends, their school friendships become particularly important as do their bonds with the schools themselves.

COLLEGE ADMISSION ADVANTAGE

The outstanding college admission record of many boarding schools prompts some families to enroll their students in order to gain an admission advantage. This strategy can have decidedly mixed results. Such a strategy is "other directed", not focused on the benefits of the boarding education per se, but on a potential outcome of such an education. As will be discussed in detail later in this book, the mere admission of a student to a high performing boarding school does not guarantee college admission success. The focus, some might call it the obsession, on college admission turns the student away from, the opportunity to develop personally, intellectually and socially and towards an outcome that is, at its basis, in the hands of others.

So too, the notion that only certain boarding schools are pathways to elite colleges is a misapprehension of college admission realities. U.S. colleges seek diversity in all its forms. The days when large cohorts of boarding school graduates were assured admission at elite universities have long passed. That said, the superior academic environment at high performing boarding schools serves as an inspiration and a springboard for students to strive and succeed.

PRESTIGE

Concurrent with college admission success, the prestige of elite boarding schools is a draw for certain students and families seeking social cachet. Such a quest is completely misguided; prestige does not derive from one's school ties. In today's world, one wonders from where it derives at all. Social benefits derived from a boarding school education include personal connections with classmates and schoolmates one would never have met otherwise and an ability to navigate amongst people from a wide variety of backgrounds who one might otherwise have never encountered. Such aspects may be advantageous but those seeking entrée to the Social Register through their school enrollment are doomed to disappointment.

ATHLETES

Athletes seeking college scholarships often enroll at boarding schools to enhance their visibility to college coaches or to further develop their skills and physical conditioning. A boarding school offers a number of advantages for the dedicated athlete. The campus itself allows for extended training and conditioning opportunities, seven days a week. Teammates and coaches are ever present.

BOARDING SCHOOL CULTURE

Some students opt for the classic boarding school experience for its own sake. Some hope to meet and befriend students from different backgrounds and countries, opportunities that may be missing from their day school and public school experiences. Many international students attend U.S. boarding schools in order to be immersed in American culture, as they study, work, play and reside with American students.

REMEDIAL ACADEMICS

Boarding schools with remedial programs attract students seeking to strengthen areas of academic weaknesses. Most schools maintain staffs of educational specialists and counselors to work with students throughout their boarding years. Because of the residential nature of boarding schools, informal tutoring and learning support from faculty, staff and other students, is readily accessible. Some schools have advanced programs for students with learning differences. Others are completely dedicated to such programs.

RELIGIOUS OR PHILOSOPHICALLY BASED EDUCATION

Boarding schools with specific religious or philosophical foundations provide students with a more complete educational context than may be found at local schools. There are numerous faith based schools operating throughout the United States, some are run by religious institutions; others are affiliated with religious groups. Virtually all are Christian denominations – with Episcopal, and Catholic schools predominant.

Some students seek schools with "progressive" educational philosophies that emphasize highly personalized and experiential learning development and eschew standardized tests and course schedules.

DAY STUDENTS

Oftentimes, a boarding school is the best educational option in its vicinity, prompting local families to send their children as day students. Day students, who live with their families at home, may be a significant factor in a school's life. Day students add some local connectivity for boarding students, with a potential circle of local friends as well as knowledge of local stores, restaurants, and points of interest.

Day student populations can have a potential negative effect at some schools, as the campus may feel depopulated on weekends when the day students are with their families at home. At other schools, there is so much going on during weekends that day students often choose to stay over in the dorms rather than go home.

CHAPTER 3
BOARDING PROS AND CONS

Boarding schools can provide an outstanding "holistic" educational experience where learning extends well beyond classroom academics to sports, extracurricular activities, and dorm life. However, boarding schools are not for every student or every family situation. The pros and cons must be considered very carefully as a critical first step.

ARGUMENTS FOR BOARDING SCHOOL

Boarding schools have traditional strengths which have been augmented by several recent societal and educational trends.

ACADEMICS

Boarding school culture is strongly pro-education. Its elite status combined with extremely low admission rates result in a motivated majority of students focused on academic success. The **quality of the faculty** of the elite schools matches and often surpasses that of many colleges. The percentage of boarding school faculty with advanced degrees surpasses that of the faculties at private day and public schools.

Boarding school classes are small, teacher-student ratios are superior, and students receive strong academic support through numerous advisors and tutors. Opportunities for educational travel, research, and independent study are abundant. Boarding education is immersive, with discussions extending beyond the classroom to conversations at meals, in activity clubs, or in the dorms. Students with high academic expectations and strong work and life habits tend to positively influence those around them. Additionally, boarding school **resources** – superior libraries, laboratories, and arts and sports facilities – offer a cornucopia of opportunities that few day schools or publics can match.

NON COGNITIVE "SOFT" SKILLS (aka CHARACTER)

Away from daily parental control, students quickly learn responsibility and self-control. Adult authority is not commingled with parent/child emotional issues. Students learn to live in close social groups and obey firm community laws. Living with other students and faculty develops social and political skills – decision making, persuasion, negotiation, and accommodation (getting along with everyone). If they have not already, students must learn self-reliance. No one will clean their rooms for them, wake them up, handle their spending money accounts, buy their clothes, schedule haircuts, or find their lost items. The schools are highly competitive but also cooperative communities, where social ease and cooperation are paired with an expectation of excellence and hard work. Confronting and then recovering from failure is another prep skill. Boarding school students often find the transition to college life a minor shift.

Like the tiny irritants that create the pearl in the oyster (more circles and ovals), the small conflicts and competitions at boarding school are integral to the development of "character", now termed "non-cognitive skills" or "soft skills". In today's test obsessed school environments, these traits are increasingly valuable. Paul Tough's 2012 book *How Children Succeed* describes traits consistent with success in life – grit, self control, zest, social intelligence, gratitude, optimism, and curiosity – all traditional prep characteristics. In a 2015 survey by the *Wall Street Journal* of nearly 900 executives "…92% said soft skills were equally important or more important than technical skills…but 89% said they have a very or somewhat difficult time finding people with the requisite attributes." A LinkedIn analysis found "the ability to communicate trumped all else, followed by organization, capacity for teamwork, punctuality, critical thinking, social savvy, creativity and adaptability."

PERSONAL SAFETY

Boarding students are shielded from certain hazards that public and day students may face in some regions. The no drive/no ride rules minimize the chances that boarding students will be involved in auto accidents, DUIs, or weekend escapades. The rules regarding off campus travel and dorm sign in/sign out, as well as 24 hour campus security and continuous adult supervision, provide more safety for students than they might have living back home.

SOCIAL BENEFITS

Boarding school communities are purposefully diverse with students drawn from every race, ethnicity, economic class, and geographical origin. Students tend to develop strong spoken and written communication skills, as well as heightened poise, assurance, and decisiveness.

Students develop strong bonds in their dorms or houses, in their sports teams, and across their boarding communities as they share their out-of-class lives together. The campus environment – competitive, high energy, group oriented – promotes personal poise, social and negotiation skills, loyalty, and confidence. The many clubs, sports teams, and service opportunities provide students with ample opportunities to discover their own strengths, talents, and interests.

COLLEGE COUNSELING

Boarding schools have developed college preparation into something approaching a science. 100% of prep school students are expected to go on to college; the focus on admissions issues is central, not a subject for a minority cohort as is the usual case in public schools. Students are trained in test taking, resume building, interviewing, and college search techniques. Since continued success in college placement is critical to the boarding school's future recruiting (in fierce competition with rival schools), the school has a deep stake in each student's admissions success.

ALUMNI CONNECTIONS

Boarding schools are noted for extensive well funded alumni associations, which serve as lifelong social clubs and business networking systems amongst alumni. The schools' alumni offices produce elaborate alumni events and reunions throughout each academic year. Each graduating class maintains officers who maintain contact information and correspond with class members. As the years pass, alumni classmates often develop deeper friendships with each other and their families, maintaining enduring class and school communities rarely found among public and private day school alumni.

Alumni status also can assist the children of alumni who seek admissions to "their" schools. Alumni who provide financial support and volunteer service to their alma maters receive preferential treatment in admissions considerations and school faculty hiring.

THE ARGUMENTS AGAINST BOARDING SCHOOL

Though boarding schools have many attractions, they are not for everyone and every family situation. Those who experience unhappy outcomes tend to be those who have not thought through the true needs of their students or their families.

FINANCIAL COST

Boarding school tuition is roughly on a par with tuition at private day schools, but the added costs of residency – room & board – make boarding school costs as high as the most expensive colleges and universities. Since college costs still loom, as may educational costs for other children, is boarding school the best option?

Also, if the student's home area offers academically acceptable private day or public schools, the rationale behind shifting to boarding school is severely weakened. If a local school's academics are on a par with boarding school levels, are the other benefits of boarding school worth the costs?

EMOTIONAL COST

A chief argument against boarding schools is the emotional price the family pays due to the student's abrupt absence. The many responses of this issue – "going away to college soon anyway", "still in contact by phone and Skype", "we can visit often" – will satisfy some families but not all. When the student goes away to school, there is a period of real sadness. This can be mitigated by the acknowledgment of what the student is gaining, but the departure is often hard on parents and siblings in multiple ways.

The student too can pay an emotional price. Homesickness is to be expected in the first weeks or months. Usually this passes as the student settles in but sometimes there are lingering emotional issues that severely hamper a student's experience. Students who are extreme introverts or socially awkward or insecure may find boarding school culture too harsh and alienating.

LIMITATIONS ON OUTSIDE ACTIVITIES

Students who maintain high level extracurricular activities, such as highly ranked athletes (playing above the high school level), professional teen actors, models, or dancers may find severe limitations due to boarding schools' intense work schedules. Such students may sometimes resolve these conflicts with special permissions or leaves of absence.

ACADEMIC STRESS AND SOCIAL PRESSURES

Stress is a real challenge at boarding school. The elite schools maintain relentless schedules and academic expectations can be very high. Boarding schools known for a more relaxed atmosphere still require more rigorous workloads than most day or public schools. Students must find ways to balance competing demands of homework, sports team practices and games, and club activities.

Socially, boarding schools are very group oriented. Students may not find much time to be alone. Gossip is endemic within these small closed communities and finding like minded friends can be a challenge. None of these issues are exclusive to boarding schools, but they tend to be amplified in the schools' close knit 24 hour communities.

COLLEGE ADMISSION LIABILITIES

Some students who are in the top decile of their run-of-the-mill public school class may find themselves ranked far lower at boarding school. Such newcomers also face the reality of competing for college admissions with high performing classmates. Additionally, boarding students from underrepresented states may lose that geographic asset for college admission, as their boarding school's location will be considered their "home state".

WHO THRIVES AT BOARDING SCHOOL?

Certain types of students can benefit greatly from a boarding school education. Extroverted students tend to do well. The numerous clubs, sports teams, and informal groupings encourage social interaction. Adaptable introverts willing to expand their experience can find new avenues to explore. Adventurous or curious students seeking to explore new interests are often well suited to boarding schools, which tend to offer a wider range of activities and academic topics than day or public schools. Many students discover passions for new areas of study and career paths, sports, and creative fields they had never before considered.

Free from the anti-intellectual bias in American teen subcultures that often dominates many public schools and some private day schools, boarding school students with a real love of learning need not mask their enthusiasms. Like-minded classmates and encouraging faculty help foster an atmosphere of excitement about academics and intellectual growth. The extensive system of academic and time management support can often help turn a lackadaisical or disorganized student into a newly empowered peak performer.

WHO STRUGGLES?

Students with ongoing emotional or psychological struggles will not find relief in boarding schools with pressured, competitive environments. Students who take offense easily or have low self esteem may not do well apart from the protection of their families. Some of these students may be ready for boarding school when they are older; some may not be ready until college; some not at all.

The most important consideration for families is not the question of whether the boarding school will accept the student; the real matter is whether this particular school, or any boarding school, is right for the student.

Students who are extreme loners often struggle at boarding school; social interaction is continual and solitude is rare. Those with low self esteem may find the competitive climate overwhelming. Conflicted students – those who have unresolved emotional or psychological issues at home – find that these conflicts accompany them to school. Students who have been forced to attend sometimes sabotage their own success as a means of protest.

Students who lack a firm command of English typically face difficulties. So do students with issues involving dyslexia, speech communication, Asperger's syndrome, autism, and language based disabilities. Some schools have excellent services for such students, but many others do not.

Students who are not sufficiently mature can also struggle. This is typical of very young students but can apply right up through the grades, as older students may have a severe imbalance between their academic and emotional maturity. If such a student is placed at boarding school solely on the basis of academic prowess, the result is rarely optimal. A student's emotional balance and maturity are stronger indicators of school success than is academic prowess.

PARENTAL CONSIDERATIONS

Applying to boarding schools is a team effort, requiring mutual understanding and cooperation. Parents are advised to carefully think through their family's readiness to move forward together.

Basic considerations include:

—Attending a boarding school is a major life change, perhaps the first of a student's young life. It will mean beginning the next phase of life earlier than other teenagers will do so.

The rewards can be many, but there are real costs to the student and the family.

—For most people, a boarding school education is not essential to one's life success. There are many roads that can take you where you want to go.

—If you are still intrigued by the possibility of a boarding school education, you might move ahead to investigating it as an option. Frame this idea as a team effort – involve everyone – and promote unity, if at all possible. If there is no general agreement to send a student to boarding school, try to achieve a general agreement to investigate – you can always cancel later on.

—Ask everyone involved – spouse, student, other children, other family members – to keep an open mind. Many people move from strongly opposed to strongly in favor once they see the opportunities and advantages of boarding school. Others charge ahead fully convinced of the benefits only to find their student balking at the last moment.

—One question to try to answer in advance: how will your student fare living away from home? In years past, American families could make a reasonably accurate prediction due to the widespread practice of sending kids off to summer camp, scouting expeditions, and the like. If these "non family" trips are not part of your student's experience, schedule some to see how she/he does with supervision by other adults but without parents. Some schools have summer programs – try those. (Note: a summer program at a boarding school is useful for the experience but gives no advantage when applying for regular admission to that school.)

—Regardless of your certainty at this point, the next task is to find the right school for your student. Not just a school that offers admission, the right school.

—Whether or not your student goes to boarding school, almost every step in this process is excellent preparation for college applications (which are coming soon enough). The school application will prompt your student to think ahead to what is needed for college applications, and as a consequence there will be more time to strengthen academic and extracurricular resumes. After the school search process, the college application procedures won't seem so daunting.

RELUCTANT STUDENT

Though some adventurous students are the first to champion going away to boarding school, many are not. They may be hesitant, or downright opposed to the idea. Young people without much world experience or self-reliance may look at such a prospect with dread. Even self-assured students who you expect to favor such a plan may balk simply because it's not their plan, it's yours – it's a matter of autonomy to reject it even if they like it!

The solution is to proceed slowly and wait for your student to make some decisions. Go ahead with some initial research (see Part II), order some catalogues, and invite your student to take a look with you and then discuss it all. Your student may get excited by the catalogues or just decide to learn more, but young people want to change their mind on their own accord and not appear as if they are giving in. Therefore, don't push anything.

Some objections that often come up.

"I will lose my friends here at home." – Response to this: "Skype and social media keep everyone in touch, and you will be back for long breaks during the school year."

"I won't know anybody there." – Response: "True, but you will soon have more friends at school than you ever did back home, and more time to see them – at sports, at clubs, and in the dorms".

"I don't like school anyway." – Response: "Boarding school teachers can inspire and help you. Classes are small and discussion based."

"What if I hate it?" Response: "Just try it for one semester (or one year). If you really want to come home after that, we can talk about that then".

However you handle objections, don't resort to arguing. You will most likely succeed by giving your student some reassurance. Also give them the power to make the final decision, as in, "We are not forcing you to go to boarding school. It is up to you to decide if you want to go. All I ask is that you take a closer look. Will you agree to visit some campuses? No commitments, no obligations. Let's just take a trip and check this out." Your objective is not to cut a deal with your student; rather, you just want her/him to consider the boarding school option. Once students have some hands-on experience – tour some campuses, meet students and teachers, and sit in on classes, and possibly sports and clubs, many will become energized to apply and attend.

If after such visits, your student remains opposed, it's best to stop the admissions quest at least for a year. Some reluctant students are actually quite wise; they seem to know somehow that they are not ready for such a major life change. This kind of student often grows into the idea of boarding school a bit later and decides to apply the following year with an eager commitment.

Some students may not want to go, but because of their family situations or the poor school options at home, they accept their parents' plan. However, if the student can't accept boarding school as necessary or good, a parent decision without student cooperation almost always ends badly. Each year, hundreds of boarding school newcomers drop out of their schools. Others tough it out and graduate, but resent their experiences and do not fully appreciate or benefit from them.

RELUCTANT PARENT

Sometimes a boarding school plan provokes a split between spouses. One parent may already convinced of the value of such an education, while the other can't imagine "losing" their child so early. This is often the case with parents without any family connections to boarding schools or parents from cultures that maintain close family ties.

The solution here is something similar to dealing with reluctant students. Parents who visit the campuses often change their minds when they see the astounding opportunities that these schools can offer their student. Reluctant parents may come to realize that their desire to keep their child home may be more about what is good for them, the parents, than what is good for the child. Such parents often make the decision, as painful as it is, to sacrifice their own happiness for the benefit of their child. This is a noble but difficult decision. The other spouse must be patient and let the process work out naturally, without trying to force a decision.

HEY, WHAT ABOUT ME? THE EFFECT ON SIBLINGS

Sometimes, the other children in the family of a prospective boarding school student feel neglected as all the focus shifts to the applicant. These siblings may turn resentful or rebellious or become withdrawn. Older children may wonder why they weren't considered for boarding schools. Younger ones, who will likely suffer more from the absence of the boarding schooler than older siblings, may feel anxious. Give them your reassurance, love and attention and try to give them an upside to this situation. More time with the parents? More space and quiet in the house? Showing the stay-at-homes some tangible benefits that may result from this boarding school quest can help get them on board with the project.

FAMILY TEAMWORK

Make this a family project. Have a group meeting to share the plan. Family time will need to be redistributed during the application process. There will also be necessary financial adjustments, as trips, tests, and tutoring costs take precedence. The older children can help with the process as practice for their own college applications. The younger ones may understand that they too might have such opportunities later on.

KEEP IT PRIVATE

As you move along considering a boarding school education for your student, keep your plans to yourselves. Announcing your intentions to your friends and neighbors can bring all sorts of negative reactions if they do not know much about boarding schools, you can anticipate such comments as:

**"Why in the world would you want to send your child away?
What did she/he do?**

or

"Well, well, you must be quite wealthy!"

or

"We're not good enough for your kid around here, is that it?"

And even if you live in an area accustomed to boarding schools, you
might be greeted with:

**"Really? The only school I would even consider sending my child to
is (fill in the blank with the name of a school other than any
you mention)"**

or

"I didn't know that your child was prep school material."

All of this sounds ludicrous and yet all of these quotes are verbatim!
The correct practice is discretion; go about your quest quietly and if
your student happens to enroll, let others know after the fact.

LETTING GO

Parents of prospective boarding students, whether they are
enthusiastic or reluctant, should know in advance that all the project
management they are about to undertake has one unavoidable result,
the gradual letting go of their maturing child.

As the application process rolls on, the student will be called to take on more and more responsibility; so too, the parent must cede responsibility. At the start, parents can order catalogues, pay for tutoring, schedule tests and so forth (in truth, it is better if the student can take on as much of this as possible). In the long run, though, the parent can't help the student write their essays or take their interviews.

Even if parents could do these things, once the student arrives on campus, parents must face the loss of their role as day-to-day supervisors. From a parents' point of view, boarding school is all about allowing professional educators to take responsibility for their children. Perhaps the most difficult aspect for parents is the sudden inability to protect their children from disappointments. Boarding schools have a lot to do with failure – in rigorous academics, on the sports fields, and in student elections. Picking oneself up again after defeat is a core lesson of prep school education, but many a parent's heart has been broken hearing their children's sorrow in tearful late-night phone calls while being unable to hug or console them.

A similar sense of loss exists when parents miss key moments in their childrens' growing lives – seeing them score a first goal or go off to a first formal dance. Though the friends your student makes at boarding school will likely be good ones, you won't meet them except on infrequent campus visits.

In essence, boarding school parents must accept their student's life changes – and their own – earlier than parents whose children stay at home until they go off to college. Some boarding school and college parents attempt to stave off such emotions by "helicoptering", hovering over their children.

Some do this with constant contact and attempts to manage or assist their students' lives. Others go so far as to buy or rent housing near campus to stay close to their kids.

Parents may feel a sense of a loss of their student's childhood, but they usually come to understand that this does not mean they have lost their child or that the boarding decision is as painful for the student as it may be initially for the parent. In time, a student's initial sense of homesickness and loneliness is healed by the excitement of new friends and the school culture. At home, parents learn to enjoy more free time and take pride in their student's boarding school adventure. Many parents are amazed when their sudents return home on breaks with more poise, maturity and confidence.

Boarding school parenting encompasses a measure of nobility and sorrow; the parent sacrifices financially and emotionally so that the child may benefit from a superior education, personal growth, and outstanding opportunities. If you and your student value these benefits despite the costs, you are ready to begin this journey.

Others will ask, "How can you let your child go to boarding school?" The parent answers, "How can I not?"

PART II -
THE SEARCH FOR SCHOOLS

The search for schools is a major task that requires effort, patience and organization. Usually the parent is managing this phase at first, but sometimes the student will undertake it. Regardless of how you begin, an important aspect of this journey is to bring the student more and more to the fore, both in putting in the effort needed to find great schools and sharing in the decision-making process.

Some students may already be leading this charge, especially if they are a bit older; other students work best in cooperation with their parents.

Both parents and students will benefit from the information in Part II.

CHAPTER 4
THE QUEST BEGINS

Applying to boarding schools has some similarities to a military campaign; before committing a major force to it, it's wise to set a strategy and then do some reconnaissance.

THE ADMISSION TIME LINE

The admission cycle does not adhere to a calendar year (January to December) nor to an academic year (August/September to June). The admission year runs mid-April to mid-April, beginning immediately after the schools have offered admission to incoming students for the next academic year. April in calendar year A begins the cycle for students planning to enter the school in the fall of year B.

BOARDING SCHOOL ADMISSIONS CYCLE

	Admission Office	**Year B Applicant**
Year A – January	Year A applications due	Student/Family considering applying for Year B; focus on grades, sports, ECs through spring term.
Year A – February	Admission committees meet	Research
Year A – March	Admission offers sent – 3/10 Revisit Days	Research
Year A – April	Revisit Days Acceptance deadlines Wait list offers go out Admission Officers take a rest!	Research Student/Family decide to apply

	Admission Office	**Year B Applicant**
Year A – May-Aug.	Wait list activity continues AOs travel	Take practice SSAT(s) at home; research schools Create initial school list Request catalogues; attend Admission events; study SSAT vocabulary words
Year B – August	End of August School year begins	Schedule AO interviews
	New application cycle (Year B)	Schedule campus visits
Year B – Sept-Dec	Campus tours	Schedule campus visits
	Applicant interviews	Begin admission essays
	More AO travel	Take SSAT
		Ask teachers for rec. letters
		AO interviews
		Campus tours
		Re-revise school list
Winter break		Complete all applications
		Complete FA forms
		Secure teacher rec. letters
		Re-take SSAT if needed

	Admission Office	**Year B Applicant**
Year B-January		Last chance uploads: essays, teacher rec. letters, fall term grades, and awards
	Year B applications due	Year B applications due A forms due
Year B – February	Admission committees meet	Possible extra campus visits
Year B – March	Admission offers sent 3/10 Revisit Days	Admission offers sent 3/10 Revisit Days
Year B – April	Revisit Days Acceptance deadlines Wait list offers go out	Revisit Days; comparative Analysis of offers; make final Decision Acceptance deadlines Wait list offers go out
Year B – May-Aug	Wait list activity continues AOs travel	Wait list activity continues Non-admits decide to hold out for wait list admit, terminate candidacy, or re-apply (Year C) Admits schedule travel Packing Summer reading list
Year B – Late Aug-Early September		Drop Off Day

The first section of the time line – through the end of the current school spring term – is the quietest. Don't skip it entirely, it has its uses. The student should keep up the Four A's – academics, athletics, arts, and activities. There's time now to enhance and strengthen areas that may be somewhat weaker than others. Spring is also a good time to collect basic information. Look at websites and catalogues. Collect information, take notes on what you – parent and student – want in a prep school. Summer is a good time for more research, academic support (tutoring) if necessary, and practice entrance examinations as well as scheduling trips to visit schools. All these aspects are discussed in detail below.

The onset of the new academic year – fall term – marks the point when applications kick into high gear. This is a very busy time. Your student may be juggling multiple school applications while dealing with typical fall term issues at the current school – new classes, teachers, etc. If you plan well, the admission process will run smoothly; the winter break allows for additional time to finish off applications, essays, etc. ahead of the application deadlines (for many schools, that's early January, for others, the end of January). If you have procrastinated, the winter break can be fraught with anxiety as the deadlines loom. It is advisable to forego a long winter break trip during the application process just to be on the safe side, in case you need the break time to properly complete applications.

If you are reading this book for the first time in the winter or spring seasons, you are well positioned to begin your admission journey for the following admission cycle. If you are reading this in the summer, you still have time to get going in the fall. If you are reading this in the fall, you have very short notice indeed. You might in this last case consider waiting until the next cycle so that your student has more time to strengthen grades and other areas.

It should be noted that this timeline is a bare minimum; many families begin earlier, some several years earlier, helping their children engage in activities that may enhance their likelihood of acceptance to boarding school several years later. Such families also make early visits to touring admission events and to the schools themselves.

ADMISSION CONSULTANTS

At this early point, it is advisable to consider whether you have the time and willingness to manage the application process yourself or if you should engage the services of professionals.

The boarding school admission journey is long and complex. Families unfamiliar with this process may be dissuaded from attempting it. Families coming to the school search in the middle of an admission cycle may also feel at a disadvantage. In such cases, professionals are available to offer their overall guidance and advice. Other pros can provide assistance to help with specific limited issues. These advisors' insights can save families a lot of time and effort.

Consultant services are usually fee based, rather than at hourly rates. Most advisors have websites that explain their services and fees, supported by resumes and testimonials from successful clients.

Admission consultants work with families and applicants on every aspect of their applications: the student's needs and interests, supervising test study, assisting with applications, advising on essays, and interview preparation. They are particularly valuable for their knowledge of the individual schools and can prepare a suggested list of schools to consider.

Typically, consultants either have extensive experience as faculty or admission officers at a boarding school themselves or have college

AO experience and have branched out to prep school consultation. Consultants can be particularly helpful when:

—Parent(s) or guardian(s) are not fully prepared to supervise the application process

—Families are completely unfamiliar with American boarding schools and their entrance procedures

—Families lack a parent with sufficient time or capability to serve as project leader to maintain the admission schedule and oversee student application progress

—Families are in internal crisis (parental conflict, parent/student conflict, financial jeopardy, other emotionally charged issues) and need a third party expert to provide objective advice

—International families seek professional leadership from consultants knowledgeable about American educational and cultural practices.

First rate consultant services are personalized and detailed; the attendant fees are significant expenditures, commensurate with this level of service. Legitimate consultants will provide explicit, comprehensive contracts clearly stating the services to be rendered and required outcomes. If the contract is insufficient in its provisions, work with the consultant to include aspects that you need. Be aware as many boarding schools have admission rates below that of most colleges; there is a significant level of risk, even with stellar students.

After cost, the second challenge is verification. The consultant business lacks industry-wide regulation or certification, and choosing can be another risk event. One suggestion would be to ask to speak with families who have recently worked with the consultant; another would be to check the consultant's credentials, past experience and current school relationships. If a consultant can't get a strong recommendation from a school admissions office, you might do well to look elsewhere.

As you will be paying a pretty penny for admission consultation, you should know precisely what you are buying. This requires a well written contract, stating services guaranteed, what outcomes you can (or cannot) expect, consultancy fees, any additional costs, terms as to how and when payment is to be delivered, terms and procedures cancelling the contract, etc.

Some consultants offer a basic package at a lower fee. A typical consultancy might provide a 60-90 minute consultation in person, by phone, or via Skype to review the student's transcript, test scores, and interests, as well as a detailed list of match schools, information about the admission process, and some advice on how to handle that on your own, followed by a second 30 minute call.

For further assurance, go with a consultant who has accreditation from known organizations. The Independent Educational Consultants Association (IECA) is the place to begin: www.iecaonline.com. The IECA maintains member guidelines, offers numerous helpful essays (though mostly for college admissions), and a list of registered consultants in a membership database.

The parent can discuss terms and conditions with the consultant by phone or email, but it's best if both the parent and the student meet with a prospective consultant in a face-to-face meeting. This is because the parent needs to confirm that the student is comfortable with the consultant and that there's a good cooperative relationship between them.

Testing centers offer practice tests held in conditions similar to the real exams – often in large classrooms with a test proctor keeping to timed test periods and rules. These services are offered on a per use basis. Scheduling is at the center's convenience and space availability. Families who wish to avoid this expense can do without it by setting up similar circumstances at home with a parent as proctor.

Tutoring can be money well spent if an applicant's subject weaknesses can be identified (practice test scores will reveal these). A tutor can analyze test answers and identify specific areas within a general subject. A tutor can also help to improve test taking skills. Improving these target weaknesses can have a significant benefit in real test results. Tutors work at an hourly rate and often can come to the family home at the family's convenience.

Professional advisors bring expertise and experience and most of all reassurance. Are they useful? Absolutely. Are they absolutely necessary in every situation? No. Most boarding school students apply and gain admission without professional assistance. It's largely a matter of what works for your family, your budget, and your student.

QUESTIONS FOR AN ADMISSION CONSULTANT

Does the consultant:

- Specialize in prep school admission? (College advising is different)

- Have extensive knowledge of boarding schools and personal contacts with school admission directors?

- Have experience and ability working with young teens?

- Does the contract state specific performance guarantees, such as interview practice and coaching, essay advising, providing a slate of schools, test preparation, and application schedule management? Are the fees clearly stated?

- Will the consultant provide a resume of recent clients and outcomes and arrange for you to speak confidentially to recent client families?

FIVE PHASE ADMISSION STRATEGY

If you choose to handle this admission project yourself, you will need a plan of action. Break down this project into five phases:

Phase 1: Assessments;
student needs/wants/assets
school wants and needs

Phase 2: School Lists;
school data gathering
create "Consider" list of schools

Phase 3: Zeroing In;
further student/school assessments
campus visits
create "Apply To" list of schools

Phase 4: Applications;
complete school applications
complete financial aid applications

Phase 5: Decisions;
schools release admission decisions
considering offers/wait lists/denials
final round of family decisions

PHASE ONE: ASSESSMENTS

To begin, carefully consider what you are looking for in a boarding school. Many students and families race through this crucial step or ignore it entirely.

Students typically frame admission as "how do I get in?" This turns the process into a game played by aspiring applicants competing to "score" an offer of admission. Books and websites abet this misguided priority. Focusing merely on admission success is shortsighted; the applicant's choice of the school is what ultimately matters. Applicants are individuals, not widgets. Each has individual needs and wants that some schools will satisfy much better than others. Knowing the needs and wants of both student and parent is essential to the school selection process.

NEEDS AND WANTS

Needs are essential aspects that will determine the student's potential for success at school. Student needs must be fulfilled – if a school does not meet a need, it is out of consideration. Some needs are general – superior academics, strong sports programs, a friendly environment. Some are specific – advanced math courses, attention deficit support or an ESL program. A first round of schools will include only schools that satisfy core needs.

Wants come into consideration later, after this first school list. Wants are attractive but non-essential aspects. They are not critical but would enhance the student's school experience. If a school's programs or culture cannot satisfy a want, this may not be a deal breaker. However, a school that can satisfy several wants will likely appeal more to a student than another school that does not satisfy them. For example, a student with recreational interests in golf and acting might gravitate more towards a school with a strong theatre program and a golf course than one without these assets.

Make a list of basic student needs – this speaks to why you, the student and parent, are applying to boarding schools in the first place. What are your most important goals? Write them down individually – the student with one list, the parent with another. Try to prioritize them, the most important need at the top, followed by the second most important. Go through all of your core needs. Is it a long list? Are all of these needs really needs, or are some merely wants?

Next, make a list of wants; you might try to prioritize them, but with wants this is more difficult, because they are not as important as needs. Never mind, just list them. The wants list matters mostly to the student, but the parent needs to know what is on the list to help in the school selection phase.

Compare the student's lists with the parents' lists. Did you agree on some needs? Did you agree on most of them? This indicates that your team is working in sync. Do you disagree on most of them? If so, more discussion among you is needed.

ACADEMIC ASSESSMENT

After thinking through your needs and wants, your next step is to honestly and fully assess the strengths and weaknesses of the student's candidacy for boarding school. The point isn't to draw judgment or conclusions from the student's record, but to identify areas that could be strengthened ahead of the application. Begin with academics.

Admission officers will look at the student's transcripts for the past several years. The most recently completed year and the current year will be given the most scrutiny. AOs pay particular attention to rigorous courses in International Baccalaureate (IB) programs, gifted programs, or Advanced Placement or Honors courses.

If the student has stellar grades in rigorous courses, one of the most demanding schools may be a good fit; a solid but not stellar student taking more standard coursework might shine at a school with a more relaxed atmosphere.

Review the student's grade point average (GPA) for the last school year and the current one. Are the grades solid As and Bs? Are there inconsistencies from term to term in the same course? Is there an upward or downward grade trend over time?

Erratic grades may suggest boredom or attention issues. An upward trend may indicate a progress in maturation. A downward trend may indicate undetected learning issues or other problems. It's wise to address erratic grade issues well ahead of the heightened work load at boarding school.

The student's current school may not provide GPAs, but if you know the letter grades, you can calculate the GPA yourself:

Letter Grade	Percent Grade	
A+	97-100	4.0
A	93-96	4.0
A-	90-92	3.7
B+	87-89	3.3
B	83-86	3.0
B-	80-82	2.7
C+	77-79	2.3
C	73-76	2.0
C-	70-72	1.7
D+	67-69	1.3
D	65-66	1.0
E/F	Below 65	0.0

TAKE A PRACTICE TEST

American and international schools vary widely in the rigor and depth of their curricula, and an analysis of coursework only goes so far in understanding a student's abilities. This is why all prep schools require an entrance examination as part of an admissions application. These tests – primarily the Secondary School Admission Test (SSAT) and the Independent School Entrance Examination (ISEE) – provide an objective measure of a student's readiness for higher schooling. The SSAT is preferred by boarding schools, though most will also accept the ISEE.

The advantage of the SSAT is that it provides a comparative measure – a student's test results are graded against the results of other test takers from previous admission cycles. Since SSAT test takers are likely applicants, the SSAT offers you a sense of how your student matches up to other applicants, not students in general.

Regardless of what test the student will take, it's a good idea to take some practice SSAT exams informally, at home. Try to create real test conditions: a quiet desk space, a timer, and following test rules. The parent can serve as test monitor. Some families administer the entire test cycle, which is about three hours long. Others just go with one section per sitting – reading comprehension, math, and vocabulary. The preferred test book is the official SSAT workbook, which has practice exams and instructions.

Go to ssat.org, the website for the SSAT test. The home page has many good resources, articles on test taking, study tips, and practice exams. There are many other resources available at outside websites such as Quizlet, IXL, and Khan Academy, as well as SSAT vocabulary apps.

Boarding schools typically list their average SSAT scores on the school websites. Knowing the student's initial practice scores can give you a better sense of which schools would be suitable. If the student aces this test without any preparation, most likely you will be looking at the highest, most elite level of boarding schools. If the student does less than great on the first try, do not worry, test taking techniques and methods of study can bring test scores up significantly. For now, practice tests help give you a sense of where the student is and what areas need to be strengthened.

Another reason for taking these early practice tests is the possibility of identifying any attention deficit or learning issues. Middle school is a time when learning issues often reveal themselves; bright students with these issues can mask them entirely during elementary school due to superior intelligence. One sign of these issues is a disparity between grades and test scores. Students who get mostly As in coursework but tank on a practice test, or those who ace the test but have erratic grades should be tested for attention deficit and learning disabilities. Another sign is disorganization and forgetfulness. These issues can be unsettling, but they are not catastrophic and can be addressed with testing, counseling, and academic accomodations.

TEST PRACTICE TIPS FOR STUDENTS

During each practice test, read the questions carefully! Answer the easy questions first, then go back for the harder ones. If you get bogged down on one question, you are burning up test time and may run out of time at the end. There is no penalty for skipping over questions, and all answers count the same. If you run out of time and miss the last four questions, what was the point of working so long on that hard one?

If you really do not know an answer, don't guess wildly. A wrong answer counts way more than not answering... but...if you are sure that two out of the four possible answers are wrong, your odds are now 50-50 if you guess between the two remaining ones. In such situations, take the chance.

Check your answers and grade. Refer to the SSAT book to get your score for the section. Unless you scored a perfect 99, take time later to analyze your test. Try to identify areas of weakness to work on. Do this with all the sections, taking them separately. Gather more information about what you need to study.

Spend some time working on the areas you need to improve. Then take the second practice test. This time take it straight through, all parts in order, with the requisite short breaks in between. Again score your test sections and overall grade. There usually is progress as you begin to get comfortable with the test procedures.

Your overall grade from these SSATs will be helpful when looking at schools. Comparing your practice scores with the SSAT averages of admitted students can give you some sense of how you will fit academically at that school in your first year.

WHAT SCHOOLS SEEK

You have thought through the student's goals (needs and wants) and academic strengths. Now it's time to consider what the schools need and want. As we have discussed, there are hundreds of boarding schools in the United States, all different from one another. Despite this, every one of these schools has common basic needs:

Money: Boarding schools are very expensive to run, even more so than colleges. Like colleges, boarding schools have admission departments, administrators managing daily school life, and an array of faculty, advisors, and support staff, but for very small student populations. Like colleges, there are facilities to maintain, a food service, sports, and extracurriculars, the whole costly gamut of residential educational expenses. Many of the older schools are on the National Historic Registry, which requires an entire extra level of regulations and costs to repair and maintain the buildings.

Where colleges and boarding schools really differ is on the income side of the ledger. Colleges have many more revenue sources than boarding schools do. Colleges run full time summer sessions; boarding schools have short term sports camps. Online courses are a growing cash cow for colleges; boarding schools don't have this income source. Colleges with significant sports programs can generate a lot of money selling broadcast rights for their sporting events; not so with boarding schools. Colleges put a lot of attention on research grants and government programs; boarding schools can't access these.

Boarding schools depend much more on tuition and alumni support per capita than colleges do. Though all these schools provide financial aid, all have limits on their resources; there is not enough money for everyone that applies for it. Consequently, at most boarding schools, as with colleges, full pay students (FP) have higher rates of admission than students requiring financial aid (FA), though this is not always the case at schools with large endowments and/or high endowment per student ratios.

Some very well off schools (very few in number) have announced that applicants from families under certain annual income thresholds can attend for free and families above that threshold up to certain limits can expect generous though partial financial aid. What isn't said is that requiring financial aid still remains a liability in some circumstances: if two applicants are roughly equal in their assets, an FP applicant has the edge over the FA student.

A vibrant school life: In order to compete with private day schools, boarding schools have to provide deeper, more intensive, more memorable student experiences. To achieve this, boarding school admission departments "build a class" of students whose skills and talents can provide this more dynamic experience.

Boarding schools need multitalented students who can make the football team, do well in class as well as write for the school newspaper and sing in the choir. In other words, great grades and high test scores are not enough for boarding school admission. Applicants have to bring talents and skills that help make the school community a better community.

College success: To a large degree, a boarding school's reputation will rest on the college entrance success of its students. This is where an applicant's outstanding academic record is very pertinent. Top performing students get into top colleges. Admitting this type of student is a boarding school priority.

In addition, there are other indications of a student's future college success that can get the schools' attention. Most boarding school applications ask if the parent went to college and where. If the parent is an alumnus/alumna of an elite college, the student might well have enhanced odds of admission to the parent's alma mater as a legacy. Other favored categories include top performing "impact athletes" (those likely to be recruited by colleges), again another fast track to college success. Students whose parents are college faculty are assumed to have an admissions advantage to that college, another attractive group for these schools.

So all this means: To get in to highly selective boarding schools, you must bring in something that those schools want – 1) high academics and/or college connections that point to your likely college admission success, 2) multiple skills and talents that will energize the campus community, and/or 3) a family history of support for the school. Some applicants can bring all three – do your best to bring at least two.

HOOKS & SPIKES

A common complaint amongst applicants is that boarding school admission is not "fair". The truth is that boarding school admission is very fair – to boarding schools. Like colleges, boarding schools are self serving, admitting students deemed most likely to significantly contribute to the schools. Despite this, many capable candidates are not chosen.

Certain characteristics are particularly attractive to schools. These characteristics, which are very few in number, are called "hooks". A hook is an applicant asset attribute that satisfies a school's need. A candidate with a hook has a significantly better chance for admission than a candidate without one, even if the second candidate has stronger overall aspects in comparison. Multiple hooks improve one's chances even more.

HOOK #1: LEGACY

The original hook was a legacy application. Schools expected to enroll the children of alumni/ae, and the majority of boarding students were legacies. The schools themselves were organized to prepare such students to survive in those colleges, not to ensure their admission to them – that acceptance was preordained.

The legacy tradition at boarding schools is an ongoing source of financial and volunteer support for the school. Legacy families tend to be reliable contributors of financial donations, volunteer service, and advocacy. Schools continue to give preference to legacies in expectation of this support, the heightened probability that the student will accept an offer of admission, and the expectation of further support when a new generation grows up to apply for admissions in decades ahead.

Nowadays, "Legacy" generally is taken to mean any applicant whose parent or grandparent attended that same school. This basic level of legacy is a so-so hook, sometimes useful, many times not. An applicant who has one or more siblings who are current students or alumni/ae of that same school are not typically considered legacies, but as many schools tend to look favorably on sibling enrollment, such applicants can be considered to hold some advantage, if perhaps less than a "true" legacy.

"Active Legacy", a student from a family with an ongoing record of service to and financial support of the school, is a much stronger hook. Best of all is the "deep prep" applicant from a family with multi-generational ties to the same school.

Legacies offer the school decided advantages. First, the school's "yield" (percentage of admitted students who then enroll) is higher for legacy admits than non legacy admits. Second, legacy students continue the chain of multigenerational family participation and financial support, a vital aspect of prep school life. These "deep preps" are often "developmental" (see below) in that these families tend to deliver significant endowments to their school, amounts sufficient to pay for the construction of new buildings and to cover on-going maintenance costs.

Historically, boarding school admits were predominantly legacy. A 1983 study from the National Association of Independent Schools (NAIS) founds that 50-70% of many school populations were legacies. As today's schools have become more academically demanding and multicultural, the numbers of legacy admits have fallen. Still, a true legacy remains a hook; a number of schools with overall admit rates below 20% report admitting 50-70% of legacy applicants; one can assume that deep prep admit rates are even higher.

HOOK #2: DEVELOPMENT

A development hook is a candidate whose family has the financial means to make significant donations to the school (for example, to fund any entire major building) AND has a record of charitable giving. Applicants from such families might well be accepted with lower statistics with an assumption that the family will convert to channel its usual largesse to help fund the school's ongoing needs.

True development cases are very rare. Merely having disposable funds is not enough; the family's demonstrated history of giving is critical. Well-to-do families lacking such a history of philanthropy would be advised to resist the temptation to simply write a big donation check to insure their student's acceptance. Such an action would likely be considered an affront.

HOOK #3: "HIGH IMPACT" ATHLETES

One traditional hook, one of the strongest, in fact, is exceptional athletic performance, termed "high impact". High impact athletes have certain characteristics:

—A history of outstanding success – highly ranked in their home states or nationally, have won individual awards or led teams to championships.

—Able to immediately join the varsity team, regardless of grade level, provide leadership, and immediately and significantly improve the team's overall success.

And therefore:

—Likely to have athletics as a hook for college applications

Boarding school coaches will be advocating strongly for a high impact player and several schools may actively seek to enroll such an applicant.

HOOK #4: URMs

Under Represented Minorities (URMs) are students from ethnic and racial minorities that are underrepresented in prep schools compared to their rates in the general population. URMs include Native Americans, African Americans, and Hispanics. As the ability to get along and understand people from different racial and ethnic backgrounds is a fundamental goal of boarding school education, URMs are sought after to help balance out an incoming class. Tracking their college admissions peers, boarding school AOs actively seek out URMs with strong school records.

An URM applicant can be either domestic or international, with both cohorts receiving favorable consideration for admission. Applicants from high income URM families have excellent chances at all US prep schools.

Domestic URMs have a significant edge over international URMs regarding financial aid. Besides the financial support available from the schools, a number of nonprofit organizations provide counseling and financing for lower income minority students. (see Appendix B – Resources)

SPIKES

In recent years a new term has arisen, namely a "spike", which can be considered a smaller, weaker cousin of a hook. As stated previously, a hook is an applicant attribute that satisfies a school's need. A spike is a more modest asset that could in certain close comparisons between otherwise equally qualified candidates help one candidate over another. For example, an applicant with an outstanding singing voice, or who has excellent but not high impact skill in a desired sport, might be said to have a spike that could favorably tip the balance in a close admissions decision.

A "hook" usually has something to do with identity – a "spike" refers to what the student does. Spikes may be candidate skills or assets that could contribute to a school community:

—Notable and verifiable experience in a business that reflects the student's passion and intellectual interests.

— Prior recognized success in robotics or coding or possibly creating apps or inventions might be considered a "spike".

— A student from an underrepresented country or state

—A student who has published or produced books, films, songs or other creative materials (not self-published)

Spikes are not tactical advantages to collect in order to game the admissions system, they are valuable as expressions of a student's central interests and abilities. Applicants tend to overrate themselves; a true spike is more than experience or success in some activity.

ADMISSION CHALLENGES

Just as some applicant characteristics enhance one's application, other aspects can limit it.

FINANCES AND FINANCIAL AID

Boarding school costs are substantial; they are prohibitive for most middle and lower income families. With annual tuition plus room and board in the $60,000 range, only very well-to-do families can afford "full pay". To address this and to provide diversity across economic strata, the schools offer considerable financial aid (FA) to offset costs. This financial aid is direct grant support, not loans. The range of families that are eligible for boarding school FA is much larger than those for college. In 2016-17, St. Paul's School offered $11.4 million in financial aid. Groton and Exeter guarantee free education to students from families with incomes of $75,000 or less, plus FA support to families with up to and beyond $200,000 in annual income.

Other top schools have similar programs, but most schools have limited funds set aside for financial aid. As most applicants apply for financial aid, the competition for admission with financial aid is much more intense than amongst full pay applicants.

This means that in most cases, FA has admissions consequences. All other aspects being equal, applicants requiring complete or nearly complete financial aid face worse admission chances from the majority of American boarding schools. For more detailed examination of boarding school financial aid, see Chapter 8: Finances.

ORMs/URMs

The term ORM stands for "over-represented minority", which itself means applicants from ethnic or racial groups whose representation in boarding school populations is disproportionately more than their proportion in the general population. ORMs on average face higher odds of admission as schools seek broad diversity, effectively limiting the numbers of any one racial or ethnic group.

Usually a student with one URM or ORM parent can self identify as a URM or ORM. URMs and ORMs can be international or domestic (US citizens or residents).

Each group faces certain common challenges. Prejudice remains a lingering issue in boarding schools. Though the overall trend is consistently towards more tolerance and acceptance, evidence of prejudice and bigotry still flare up, as they do in the larger community. Most schools now have diversity staffers and often entire departments charged with educating students and providing counseling.

Surrounding localities may not be so tolerant. Boarding school diversity brings students of races and ethnicities with which local residents may not be familiar. Town/gown incidents sometimes involve bigotry and prejudice. This too is on the wane, as minority populations become more common in areas where formerly they were scarce or nonexistent.

Statistically, ORMs outperform all other cohorts in both GPAs and admissions testing. As a consequence, ORMs on average must perform significantly better to admission results similar to students from other groups.

A century ago, the number one ORM was Jewish students, whose academic skills and percentage of applications relative to the overall Jewish population were considered negatives. Those who were admitted had to demonstrate qualities significantly superior to their non-ORM (i.e., WASP) competitors. This bias has gradually lifted over many decades.

Today ORMs are generally understood to mean Asian students, both domestic and international. This is problematic in numerous ways.

First, Asian Americans tend to be lumped together with international students from Asia, though these two groups have completely different issues and characteristics. Second, the term "Asian" is a catchall which lumps together everyone from Asian descent, be they Filipino, Thai, or from another country of origin.

Asian American students are often native born and completely American in their lifestyles and assumptions. Their families may be native born or immigrants, but all have direct and often long term experience living in the United States.

INTERNATIONALS

International students are a growing cohort at American boarding schools, which has reduced admission chances for individual students. From 2006-2016, international students in the US (university and high schools) grew by 73% with China accounting for nearly 60% of overall international student growth over the past decade and 31.2% of all foreign students in the US, a total of 328,547 in 2015-2016. 60% of all foreign students come from four countries: China, India, South Korea, and Saudi Arabia. (Sources for above statistics: ICEF *Monitor*: Intl. Consultants for Education and Fairs, May 2016 and Project Atlas, Institute of International Education).

International students may face cultural and language challenges at American boarding schools. As their families live far away, internationals may suffer from a lack of regular contact and support.

Though there are exceptions, internationals tend to be full pay (FP) applicants. Financial aid for international students is not impossible but it is atypical.

GEOGRAPHY

As is the case with college admissions, boarding schools strive for geographic balance; when many applicants derive from the same location, that location becomes a liability. This means that New England applicants applying to New England schools are somewhat disadvantaged. New York students will be somewhat enhanced applying to schools well away from the New York region.

WHEN TO APPLY

One of the most distinctive aspects of boarding schools is the lack of mandatory ages for grade levels; students can enter at a grade level that the family and the school agree are appropriate for the student. This freedom requires consideration of how each grade level may impact the student.

Entering in 8th or 9th grade – In the past, many boarding schools began at eighth grade level; now only a few do. Most begin at 9th grade. Either way, students coming in at the lowest grade level receive considerable academic support as the schools ease the students into advanced academics. In this first year, homework assignments are shorter and less frequent, and study hall sessions are scheduled, mandatory, and overseen by faculty or student proctors. These younger students receive more advising and there are more rules. The challenge is that boarding school life at thirteen or fourteen may not be suitable to many young people who lack self confidence or emotional maturity for their age. The advantage is that the students bond sooner and tend to be the school leaders later because they are involved in teams and clubs ahead of students that enter school at a higher grade.

Entering after the school's initial grade level presents challenges, not the least of which is a diminishing supply of available places that the school needs to fill. There are fewer spots in 10th grade, fewer still in 11th, and very few if any in 12th. Students entering at the higher grades also are expected to bring skills and assets useful to the school – in coursework, sports, arts, and activities. These demands rise with each higher grade.

Entering in 10th grade after a year of high school elsewhere allows the student to mature ahead of leaving home for boarding school. However, entering tenth graders often experience an academic shock when confronting boarding school academics. Schools tend not to offer entering tenth graders the kind of support that the younger students receive; this tends to result in more of a sink or swim situation, as the new tenth graders must deal with less academic support while adjusting to living away from home.

Entering in 11th grade tends to be a transition similar to an entering tenth grader's, but with one year less at the school, the entering eleventh grader may be at a disadvantage in making friends, gaining leadership positions, and preparing for college admissions. Eleventh grade in boarding schools also tends to be most rigorous academically.

Entering in 12th grade or as a post graduate (PG) tends to be the domain of athletes already accepted onto teams, with boarding school way station to college. Friendships and connection with the school can be limited; success with this strategy often lies in making close contacts through sports teams and club activity. Some 12th grade or PG newcomers do come in primarily for academic goals.

Entering as a Repeat – One characteristic of a boarding education is the option of repeating a grade. Students can repeat at any grade level, allowing them more time to get settled at school, strengthen their academics and athletics and allow for more time for leadership positions and friendships. Many boarding schools have 20-30% of their students as repeats. Under certain circumstances, repeat years may negatively affect NCAA athletic eligibility and/or National Merit Scholar eligibility.

STUDENT QUALITIES THAT SCHOOLS SEEK

There is no mystery to what qualities the schools are looking for in prospective students – these qualities are seven in number. They begin with the Four A's: academics, athletics, arts, and activities, plus three more.

Academics - Schools want students who have an academic record that indicates that they will succeed in course work and tests. The more selective the school, the better the applicant's record should be, with rigorous courses and excellent grades and test scores.

Athletics – Boarding schools seek solid to outstanding athletes in the sports that the school maintains; being an outstanding cricket player will likely not help you at most American boarding schools. Prep schools have different sports in three seasons – fall, winter, and spring. An ideal sports resume would demonstrate success in at least two sports in two different seasons.

Arts – The arts, especially the performing arts, hold a place of high regard at these schools. The boarding campus needs performers – musicians, actors and dancers.

Activities – Boarding schools want students who can serve as a news reporter, campus tour guide, cheerleader, yearbook photographer or some other contribution to the social and cultural life of the school. Make sure at least one of your activities is one of these school enhancers.

Service – The schools look at community service as a necessary aspect of character building. Students who demonstrate an ongoing dedication to social awareness – through charity work, church outreach, scouting, or volunteering – will get the schools' attention.

Leadership – The above activities are important, but leadership in those activities is even more so. The schools seek to select and develop students with leadership abilities or potential: team captains, club officers, volunteer leaders, and student government standouts.

Non Cognitive Skills (aka Character) - Increasingly, schools are paying close attention to students who demonstrate "soft skills" such as cooperation, negotiation, persistence, and ethical and emotional intelligence. The Enrollment Management Association (the professional organization that administers the SSAT) collaborated with thirty-two schools to develop a Character Skills Assessment which was put into service in 2017.

If the student's resume already includes four or five of these categories, you are ready to apply. If there are three or less, it would be wise to strengthen the resume before applying. Students from families that are familiar with prep school admission (and college admissions as well) often begin to work on all these categories in elementary school. By the time they reach the seventh and eighth grades, such kids are already strong candidates and often sail through with many offers of admission.

Part of your calculation is a matter of where you are in the admission cycle. You might be reading this in November, two months away from the application deadline. If so, it's probably too late to make many improvements in your student's resume. If not, what can be done?

One option is to just go ahead, apply and see what happens. Not every student is strong in all seven areas, and most do get in with less than perfect resumes. So why not your student? Second, if your student doesn't get good results, one option is to just stay put, work on improving areas that need improvement, and re-apply after a year or even two while your student builds up skills. The categories cited above are consistent assets for boarding admissions, but they are not the whole story. Admissions officers (AOs) are looking beyond these basics when selecting individual students.

Boarding school AOs, like their college peers, have one overarching objective – to select a strong vibrant class from the pool of applicants. But "building a class" for boarding schools is much different than doing so for college. This is chiefly due to population numbers. Colleges tend to be enormous compared to these schools. Boarding School Review lists only fourteen schools with a thousand or more students. The large majority of colleges are many times that number.

With these large numbers, college AOs can seek specialists – outstanding scholars, athletes, artists, and scientists- to populate their campuses.

Boarding schools have no such option, even at the largest of them. There are not enough places to admit specialists, except in the case of highly skilled athletes. Instead, schools seek students who are multi talented – strong across the board. Without these, the schools would not be able to maintain their multiple sports teams, produce their plays and musical events, or manage and write for their publications while maintaining high academic standards. Boarding school applicants who have multiple talents can therefore take heart that their skills will get noticed. However, there is a downside: the schools often seek to fill the gaps they need to fill, needs which change year to year. An outstanding hockey goalie may be of immense interest to a school that needs one, but not so much to a school that already has three. Because of this, boarding school admissions are never a sure thing. It's a dance between what you offer and what the school wants.

The small student populations at these schools brings another aspect to the admissions process, that of personality. Boarding schools are small communities. Students who bring a cheerful, positive disposition, who are good in groups, and who are inclined to volunteering are prized. So is enthusiasm. That is why an applicant's record of participation in clubs and service organizations is important and why the impact of the student's interview is particularly so.

Does the student play a sport at a high level? If not, how about a record of continuous participation in a sport for several years? Either should be considered an asset. If the answer is no to both, is there time to begin a sport that the schools offer? Informal jogging or swimming several times a week has promise – virtually all schools have track and cross country teams and many have swimming programs.

Student experience with a core school club is always helpful. Such clubs include student publications, especially the newspaper and yearbook; band and singing groups; and school spirit organizations. Academic clubs are also assets such as the National Honor Society, Key Club, etc. Personal interest clubs – investment club, entrepreneur club, chess, cooking, robotics – help reveal the student's personality. Some students put considerable focus on clubs, service, sports, and arts not connected with their schools. Scouting, church groups, and outside clubs and projects will all be of interest to school admissions officers.

Keep a detailed log of all applicant activities, in school and out, by grade level. Do not rely on memory. Create a document and add new awards and achievements as you go along. This will be very useful when the time comes to fill out applications. Work with the Student Assessment Check List to get you started.

A clear understanding of the student's strengths and weaknesses is needed now. The goal here is to target areas that can be strengthened and areas of activity to be added. After thinking through all of these issues, you are now ready to move on to the first major campaign of your admissions quest – the search for schools.

STUDENT ASSESSMENT CHECK LIST:

Category List	Strong? Yes/No	To Do
GPA – Most recent full year – Current year to date		
COURSE RIGOR		
PRACTICE SSAT SCORES – Individual scores – Overall score		
ATHLETICS – Sport #1 – Sport #2		
SCHOOL EXTRACURRICULARS		
OUT OF SCHOOL		
EXTRACURRICULARS		

Category List	Strong? Yes/No	To Do
SERVICE		
LEADERSHIP		
ESSAY WRITING		
INTERVIEWING		
HOOKS?		
SPIKES?		
ADDITIONAL ASSETS		

CHAPTER 5
YOUR FIRST SCHOOL LIST

Once your family has made the decision to move forward, Admissions Phase Two – the search for schools – begins in earnest.

Applying to boarding schools is time-consuming but relatively straightforward. (Chapter 7 will walk you through that process.) Deciding on which schools to choose is much more difficult. Some schools that look very similar in terms of their statistics can have vastly different cultures. Comparing one to another and then to thirty more can be a bewildering exercise without planning and organization.

STUDENTS: NEED MORE TIME? HERE'S HOW TO FIND IT

School applications suck up a lot of time. You are already booked 24/7! Where will you find the time to do this? It can't be academics, sports, or extracurriculars. You need those for your applications. So where, then? The obvious place is the center of your universe - your cell phone. All that time on Instagram and Twitter has gotta go. All that time playing video games, shopping, chatting. All out. You might as well get used to it. You will have no time for that stuff at boarding school.

If you can wean yourself from cell phone addiction to focus on this great task, you are taking a big step towards maturity and responsibility whether you go to prep school or not. Your grades will improve, your college chances will improve, and guess what? – there will still be time for fun stuff. Eliminating techno-addictions makes your life better.

PARENTS: MAKE PLANS TO SUPERVISE

It would be wonderful if the student could completely manage this application process. Wonderful, but unlikely. Many students applying to prep schools are eighth graders, and some are starting to work on their applications at the seventh or even sixth grade level. Students so young can't manage the entire process on their own. Some adult oversight from parents, guardians, and/or professional consultants is required. Parents or guardians should assume that they will need to put time in, either to take on the entire task or to supervise and to step in directly when something goes awry.

If yours is a two-parent household, it's usually more efficient to have one parent designated as the project manager. Boarding school applications have many deadlines and details; splitting up the parental management can create more complications – miscommunications, missed deadlines, or dropped assignments.

Two tasks require direct parental responsibility. The first is budgeting the application costs – travel, study material costs, application and testing fees, and shipping/mailing. The second is scheduling travel for campus visits. If your family income is below a certain threshold, many schools will provide application cost support such as fee waivers and the like, but you will need to apply. (See the Financial Matters section for more information). If you have other children that you suspect may go down this boarding school road, take some comfort; all this gets somewhat easier with siblings who are coming up after.

ORGANIZATION

The search for schools can be a fun family project; it can also be a big headache if approached haphazardly. This may be the most complicated undertaking the student has yet faced. Well organized students will be challenged; less together kids can quickly be overwhelmed by the complexities. As discussed previously, American boarding schools are independent entities (very independent!). Each has its own ways of doing things, with different requirements, deadlines, and procedures. Managing all these details requires organization.

To that end, your second task is to create *data collection systems*. Make an office space in your home reserved for this project. Create separate files – digital and hard copy- for each school that interests you. In the beginning this may blow up to twenty or thirty school files. It's a good idea to have the student handle this step, to own the process. If that's not working, the parent can step in to get things rolling.

A filing cabinet with drawers and hanging files works very well. You can get away with a cardboard version. Yes, this is old school, but you need a reliable shared system; hard copy lists, logs and files have their uses. Each school gets a file where you store course catalogues, FAQ sheets, hard copy correspondence, and other paperwork.

Create a daily journal – and use it! Log every email to/from a school and every letter sent or received. Any event that impacts admissions should be noted, including who was involved, what was discussed, any outcomes, and follow-up notes.

Keep a large paper calendar dedicated to your admission quest. Write in dates for SSAT tests, admissions fairs, interviews, and campus visits. If you anticipate applying to multiple schools, this calendar can fill up quickly; it's useful to have a visual display of a full month's scheduling.

Use individual admissions checklists for each school. Some schools create these themselves which you can print out. You may have to create your own for other schools. These checklists are easy to ignore – don't! Even if you are applying to only one school, it's very easy to forget what you have done or need to do. When you are juggling multiple applications, things can get crazy. Checklists can help keep you sane.

SCHOOL SEARCH COMMUNICATION

Email account - The admissions process generates a lot of correspondence – questions about the school, questions about application procedures, scheduling visits; the list is long. To manage all this, it's a good idea to create a new, dedicated email account, with both student and parent having access to it. This keeps everything in one place with less likelihood for getting lost in the avalanche of emails in a regular account. Check these emails frequently, especially if you end up applying to several schools.

Social Media - Be aware that a student's presence on social media may be subject to scrutiny by some schools during the decision-making process (after the application has been submitted). This could be an issue if student applicants have posed for photos or shared questionable materials on easily accessed sites. Students who have such posts are advised to take them down ahead of applying to schools. Instead, a student can put some positives up there – photos of student awards, video clips of sports or school shows, interesting trips, or creative work. Parents and students are advised to discuss this ahead of formal applications.

Student Follow-up - Following up is one critical communications step which can get overlooked. It is very easy to forget to do this step. Keep track!

After every encounter with an admissions officer from a school that interests you – at an interview, on campus, or at a prep school fair – the student should follow up with a handwritten note on good stationary. Prep school manners remain very old school; an emailed thanks is a weak substitute for a real letter. Send another follow-up to the Dean of Admission. Thank-you notes after interviews and tours demonstrate serious interest in the school and will set the student apart from the rest of the applicant pack. A failure to follow up suggests a lack of interest in that school.

Personal Contact Rules - The more a school sees an applicant in person, the stronger that young person's presence will be felt when the time comes to choose between applicants. The student should make every effort to attend school fairs and receptions and take any opportunity to meet face to face with school representatives. Ask the school for alumni or parents near you. Even faraway internationals should do this. American boarding schools regularly tour Europe, Asia, and Latin America, and alumni and parents are available to meet with you. An added plus is the stronger sense of confidence and poise that the student will develop from repeated social encounters with adults.

AND WHILE WE'RE ON THE SUBJECT OF SOCIAL ENCOUNTERS

When budgeting for this admission process, consider scheduling some training for your student in social etiquette. Learning how to greet adult strangers, introduce oneself and others, shake hands firmly, as well as how to make eye contact and carry on polite conversation, are skills best learned ahead of all important admission interviews. Some parents, especially in the southern states, go the whole distance by signing their students up for Cotillion courses (they get dance and dining lessons as well). One time meet and greet sessions are another alternative. This might seem to be overkill or trivial. It would be if your student is socially adept, self assured, and comfortable in adult company. If not, this suggestion could mean the difference between an acceptance and a rejection. Boarding schools value poise and social skills, which take practice.

BOARDING SCHOOL CATEGORIES

As with colleges, boarding schools are subject to endless variations of "Top School". This obsession is sad in the college world; in the prep world it is silly. These schools are so widely divergent in their particulars that rankings make sense only to those who are outside the community. One common list rates five well known schools in an arbitrary order of fabulousness. The implication of such a ranking is that admissions to Number One would be best, with admission to Number Two second best and so on. Yet two of these schools have student populations of over a thousand, some are less than half that size, some are close to urban centers, some are quite remote, some are religiously oriented, others not, etc. The ranking of such schools might appear to make sense to the uninitiated. The reality is that students may encounter radically different experiences. What is the point of sending a student to a great school if that student hates it and does poorly as a result?

Boarding schools can be categorized in multiple ways. Any one school will likely fall into several categories.

ELITE SCHOOLS

Elite schools are characterized by demanding academics, high endowments, generous financial aid, advanced resources, high SSAT and SAT/ACT scores, strong college placement and very low acceptance rates. Elite schools can be high pressure competitive environments. There is no one official list of elite schools nor are there agreed upon metrics for evaluations/comparisons. Elite schools tend to cluster in New England, with some in the Middle Atlantic region and in California.

Schools with low admission rates (20% and under) include Cate School (CA) , Choate Rosemary Hall (CT), Deerfield Academy (MA),

Groton School (MA), Hotchkiss School (CT), Lawrenceville School (NJ), Middlesex School (MA), Milton Academy (MA), Phillips Academy, known as Andover (MA), Phillips Exeter Academy (NH), St. Paul's School (NH), Thacher School (CA) and THINK Global (offices in NY).

Schools with admit rates between 20-30% include Berkshire School (MA), Blair Academy (NJ), Brooks School (MA), Concord Academy (MA), Georgetown Preparatory School (MD), Governor's Academy (MA), Hill School (PA), Hockaday School (TX), Loomis Chaffee School (CT), Noble & Greenough School (MA), Peddie School (NJ), St. Andrew's School (DE), St. George's School (RI), Taft School (CT), Suffield Academy (CT) and Westminster School (CT).

"HIDDEN GEM" SCHOOLS

Hidden Gems are characterized by quality academics and campus life, somewhat relaxed admission rates, strong financial aid and less public and media attention than the elite schools receive. Hidden Gems often have less pressured campus cultures, excellent faculty, student support and college outcomes, and a variety of learning styles including support for learning disabilities. Hidden Gems can be found in every region of the United States.

COED SCHOOLS

Most boarding schools moved to coeducation in the 1970s. Some single sex schools merged; many all boys schools added girls. Coed campuses provide more opportunities for social interaction and a variety of relationship with the opposite sex. Parents with girls seeking coed schools should evaluate school cultures carefully. Some schools offer full parity between girls and boys; other schools tend to favor boys in ways overt or subtle.

SINGLE SEX SCHOOLS

Once the norm for most boarding schools, single sex schools are now an alternative choice. The pros for single sex schools are several. Girls often find more academic support and encouragement without boys around; boys can bond with no need of proving themselves to the girls. Single sex schools are known for strong financial aid, the girls schools in particular – all top twenty schools with the highest percentage of students on financial aid are girls' schools.

Single sex schools often have strong programs for students with learning differences. Both sexes report less social pressures without issues of campus romances and dating. Single sex schools are typically matched, with "sister" and "brother" schools hosting dances and other events. Well known boys' schools include the Avon Old Farms and Salisbury schools in Connecticut, and the Phelps School in Pennsylvania. Girls' schools include the Annie Wright School in Washington, Foxcroft and St. Margaret's schools in Virginia and St. Timothy's School in Maryland.

TRADITIONAL SCHOOLS

These schools are known for a formal dress code (typically coat and tie for boys, dresses for girls, some schools require school blazers), daily chapel attendance and seated dining. "Modern" schools do not have a formal dress code, use cafeteria style dining and do not have daily chapel. Some schools intermix the two styles.

RELIGIOUS BASED SCHOOLS

These typically have a religious study component in coursework, and daily or weekly religious services. Religious schools vary widely in the religious focus on campus. An array of faiths and denominations maintain prep schools with – Episcopal, Catholic and Nondenominational Christian having the most school affiliations.

MILITARY SCHOOLS

Boarding schools with military traditions have a long history in the United States. These tend to be single sex (all boys). Well known military schools include Valley Forge Military Academy in Pennsylvania, Saint Johns Military School in Kansas and Admiral Farragut Academy in Florida; Indiana's Culver Military Academy has a sister school, Culver Girls' Academy.

PRE-PROFESSIONAL ARTS SCHOOLS

Some schools feature exceptionally strong arts programs for students focused on careers in the arts. These includes the Walnut Hill School (MA), the Idyllwild Arts Academy (CA) and Interlochen Arts Academy (MI).

ADD/ADHD/LD SUPPORT

Many schools provide support for students with attention deficit (ADD/ADHD) or learning differences. Some of these include the Proctor Academy and Tilton School in New Hampshire, the Dunn School and St. Catherine's Academy in California, the Hun School of Princeton and Pennington School in New Jersey, San Marcos Academy in Texas and Kings Academy in Tennessee. Some schools specialize in such programs, such as the Purnell School for Girls in New Jersey, the Forman School in Connecticut and the Vanguard School in Florida.

JUNIOR BOARDING SCHOOLS

Junior Boarding Schools (JBS) enroll students in pre high school grades. Some are affiliated with boarding high schools such as the

Cheshire Academy and St. Thomas More School in Connecticut, and the Ojai Valley School and Southwestern Academy in California. Other JBS bridge between middle and high school grades, such as the Eaglebrook, Fay and Fessenden schools in Massachusetts.

POST GRADUATE STUDY

Many schools offer this option, an added year of study after high school graduation but before college. The Bridgton Academy in Maine specializes in PG study.

SCHOOL SIZE

Large schools and small schools can feel very different. Large schools are more diverse, with a wider range of students, more faculty, more course choices, more clubs. Athletics at the larger schools tend to be better, with deeper teams and specialists brought in for the major sports. Students with a wide range of interests will typically find other students with similar interests. There's a college-like feel to large boarding campuses. The downside of all this is a certain sense of anonymity some students feel. A school with a 1000 plus student body may seem less personal and friendly to some. A tight bond amongst classmates and alumni can be more difficult to achieve than at smaller schools.

Small schools are by their nature intimate; it's easier to get to know most everyone. There's a sense of closeness and belonging. Perhaps too much at times. Small school alums often mention that their small schools can feel very small after two or three years with the same tightly knit community and privacy is harder to come by when everyone knows everything about everyone else. The small student body means that the range of courses and clubs is necessarily smaller than at the large schools and the smaller pool of student athletes often means that the quality of the sports teams is weaker (this is most certainly not true in every instance). Small schools tend to have stronger student and alumni bonds than the larger schools.

LOCATION AND ACCESS

A school's location is not incidental to the selection process. The eager applicant, once enrolled, becomes a resident living in one place for months and often years on end. *Climate:* The classic New England school offers dazzling autumn colors followed by freezing slate grey months and a short vibrant spring season. Long New England and Midwestern winters drive students indoors for long stretches, unless they're up for outdoorsy activities like skiing and skating. The Mid-Atlantic schools offer similar but somewhat milder climate issues. Southern schools have many months of sun and humidity; Western schools also feature longer stretches of sun with low humidity and cooler nights. *Urban/suburban/rural settings*: There are few options if you are looking for an urban environment. Most boarding schools have secluded campuses, some in remote locations. Is the nearby town accessible on foot or by bike? Are there cafes, restaurants, and stores? Off campus cinemas and cultural options? *Local communities:* Are the locals friendly to the school and its students? Is the local community multiracial/multiethnic or homogenous?

Access simply means the ease or difficulty of getting to and from the school. In this matter, the student and the family may have different agendae. From the student's point of view, access from home to school and back may not be so important. The student will likely be making that trip only a few times each calendar year. What the student might focus on is weekend trips – to a mall, a big city, or a vacation destination.

Families have other criteria. If the family intends to be involved with the student's life and the school, a number of family trips might be in the offing – parents' weekend, trips to sporting events and performances, and other campus community events. With these considerations, the distance from the family home to the school or complex travel connections can come into play.

Local families usually have day students though some local students are boarders, either for the boarding experience or for admissions reasons (schools sometimes have more places available for boarders than day students).

Close distance families live at some distance from the school, far enough that the student must board, but close enough that the family can come to campus by car, train, or bus for sporting matches, performances, school wide events, and any emergency. The actual distance varies according to the family and circumstances, but usually travel is by car with a travel time of one half to two hours one way.

Far distance families live far from campus – a plane, train, or road trip of many hours. These families must expend extra effort and expense to get to campus. They usually make the trip infrequently. The student may take a school vacation with a friend's family. Far distance families have to take bad weather into consideration – times when snow, rain, or wind could prevent travel to or from the school.

International students usually go home only at the end of the school year and perhaps for the winter break. All other school breaks are spent with other students' families or with family friends or relatives.

Both far distance and international families should consider adequate airport access and the availability of direct flights. This takes extra research, as most American airports do not offer direct service to many countries.

Transportation is a major access issue for any family seeking regular campus visits and needs to be considered carefully. Another access issue is cell phone/internet service. Some schools suffer from poor cell service due to thier locations.

SCHOOL RESOURCES, DATA & CHARACTERISTICS

As you research schools, you may want to consider the following:

ENDOWMENT

A school's financial health is largely based on its endowment – the funds separate from operating budgets that can be used for financial aid grants, physical plant expansion and other long range, high cost undertakings. Those with meager endowments may be vulnerable to future financial problems.

FINANCIAL AID DATA

Families seeking financial aid would do well to review these numbers closely: annual financial aid totals; average financial aid package; percentage of students awarded financial aid. Schools vary widely in how they distribute financial aid. Some keep aid to a limited number of "hooked" students, such as athletes. Some schools with deep pockets offer aid to a wide range of family incomes, including an upper range that would be excluded at other schools. Many schools have FA estimators on their websites (see Finances, Chapter 8).

STUDENT SUPPORT SERVICES

You should be clear about the school's student support system – dorm supervisors, academic councilors, student prefects or proctors, parent organization volunteers.

If your student requires additional support, investigate such services ahead of applying: tutoring and remedial programs, psychological-emotional counseling, physical training and/or therapy, time management/organization counseling.

TECHNOLOGY

If your student leans towards tech subjects and projects, this is an area to investigate. Is the school's IT current or lagging? Does the school offer advanced tech learning and project opportunities? Are the students mentored and led, or are they ahead of the faculty in tech areas? Tech quality is surprisingly erratic from campus to campus.

ESL

International students may want to find schools that offer English as a Second Language (ESL) programs with specific orientation programs for internationals. Though ESL programs are widespread, not all schools offer them.

SSAT SCORES

Average or mean SSAT scores are gathered from entering students from the past several years. These numbers can give you a sense of the intellectual intensity of the student body and some sense of where you or your student will be positioned within the entering class during the first year at school.

DIVERSITY

These statistics give a sense of the range of student backgrounds by religion, gender, ethnicity, race, and national origin. Schools with wide diversity offer more opportunities to learn about different people. Schools with extreme imbalances (too large a cohort or too small) may be of significance, according to your priorities.

CLASS AND FACULTY STATISTICS

Boarding schools are known for small class size and superior teacher to student ratios, but it is always wise to check individual school data to corroborate such assumptions. Are all classes of a similar size or are there tutorials with one-three students and/or larger lecture style courses?

Faculty data help you keep a better sense of a school's learning environment. How many teachers are there per student? How many have advanced degrees in their fields? At what level of such degrees? What percentage of faculty lives on campus? What are the average number of faculty living in a dorm?

DAY STUDENT PERCENTAGES

Day students have a decided effect on the personality of boarding schools. The range of day students at the schools is wide, from none to a large majority. The presence of day students may have both salutary and negative consequences.

Day students often act as guides for their boarding peers, with recommendations for local restaurants, shops, and sightseeing. Day students know how to get to airports and trains and usually can help with travel plans to nearby cities. The families of day students are valued as volunteers, often helping out at school events, dorm parties, and sporting events. Day families invite boarders over for weekends and end of term holidays; they can serve as parent substitutes in times of crisis or stress.

Day student populations may present some issues for boarders. Some schools have a deserted lonely feel on weekends when day students leave. However this can be mitigated if nearby towns are lively and accessible to the boarders. Also, day students at some schools may lack the broad diversity of boarding students in terms of class, race, ethnicity, and/or life experience.

TEACHING STYLES

Most schools use the Harkness (conference table discussion system) but how this method is used and how effectively may have widely differing outcomes. Does the school use Harkness in all classes? Most? Some? Are the school's teachers specifically trained in Harkness methods? Is there a true student discussion based learning environment or do traditional teacher lecture practices prevail? Are there innovative teaching practices and technologies in use?

HEAD OF SCHOOL

The Head of School can have a significant impact on a school environment. What is the Head's educational background, educational philosophy, and leadership experience? Has the Head articulated a long range plan and what is it?

CURRICULA

Details of curricula, graduation requirements, options for honors, AP, IB, electives, independent study and capstone courses can typically be found in course catalogues on school websites.

If the student is advanced in some course work, you will want to find out if individual schools can provide advanced study options. The school's admission office can steer you to the right person to answer specific academic questions.

CAMPUS

The size of campus and any unique features may be of importance. Are there woods, gardens or other natural areas that students can access? Are religious services held on campus? What faiths? Are religious ministers on staff or affiliated with the school? If there is a regular morning chapel service? Is it a daily service? Is student attendance required? Is it faith specific or ecumenical?

Is the school library professionally staffed and adequately stocked with research materials? Are there other research resources at the school or at other institutions nearby? Some schools have outstanding student opportunities for clubs, service, social events, off campus trips, and travel.

CONDUCT

Rules of student conduct, discipline and judiciary procedures: does the school have student disciplinary committees as well as faculty/ administration committees? Does the school have a "One Strike" or a "Two Strike" policy? "One Strike" means that a single major misbehavior will result in expulsion. "Two Strike" allows probation but not dismissal on the first incident.

THIS ISN'T SHOPPING

As you progress with your school search, take care to remember what you are seeking. Boarding students sometimes find themselves on the right campus for the wrong reasons. "What's in it for me?" does not serve well in the long run. This isn't shopping and you're not buying a school, you are looking to join one. A boarding school education is not a commodity or a transaction; it is a community, a relationship.

ADMISSION STRATEGIES

It makes sense to develop a specific strategy for your school search. If you already know what you want, you can look at schools according to your criteria. If you are new to the boarding world, you may want to explore more before settling on a strategy. Some strategies include:

GO BIG OR GO HOME

Some applicants have good school choices at home. They are applying only to the most elite boarding schools. If they do not get in, they will stay at their present school. This strategy is simple and stark – either the student has the academic statistics or not, either the school(s) offer admission or not. Those relying on this "all or nothing" approach can easily find themselves shut out entirely.

GO WIDE

Some applicants choose to apply to a range of schools – those with very low admission rates and those with moderate and high admission rates – to better the prospects for offers of admission. The trick here is not merely to find schools that will offer admission but to find schools that the student will be happy to attend.

"Going Wide" is a popular strategy for those families seeking substantial financial aid. Of three schools offering admission, possibly only two, one or none may offer enough aid to allow the family to accept a place. A wider range of target schools may result in more options for such families.

GO NEARBY

Schools that are not too far away allow families to visit for sports, performances, and other school events. If this is important to you, decide on a maximum distance or driving time to determine how far away a school on your list can be. Families living in New England or the mid-Atlantic states have many school options close by. Families in other areas and internationally have much more limited options.

REACHES-MATCHES-SAFETIES

Many students applying to colleges use a system known as "Reaches-Matches-Safeties". The easy admit colleges are known as **Safeties**. A Safety is a college with student statistics lower than the applicant's, where admission is certain or nearly certain, costs are affordable, and that the applicant would like to attend if other options fail. A **Match** is a college that has comparable statistics to the applicant's, where admissions chances are good, costs are affordable, and that the applicant would like to attend if options for Reach colleges fail. A **Reach** is a college with higher statistics than the applicant's and with a low admit rate, a college which presumably the applicant would choose to attend if accepted.

Boarding school applicants who use this system do so to their disadvantage. This is so because boarding school academics are decidedly different from college academics. The reality of college academics is that elite college academics are no more difficult overall than academics at many less selective colleges. The problem with elite colleges is getting into them, not handling the course work once accepted.

Not so with boarding schools. The most selective schools are the most difficult. If the student "squeaks in" to an elite school, they likely will face a very tough time keeping up with the academics, which are designed to become more difficult year after year. "Reaches, matches and safeties" for boarding schools is a very bad idea.

BIG FISH/SMALL POND

One strategy is to seek a school where the applicant's grades and SSAT scores are at the high end of that school's student statistics, thereby increasing the student's chances for academic ranking and student leadership opportunities. Such students understand that, as regards both personal satisfaction and college admission success, mere attendance at a tippy top famous school, struggling in the middle or the lower third of a class, is not nearly as advantageous as thriving within the upper third or quarter of a class at a good but not so famous school.

STEPPING BACK

A variation on the big fish/small pond strategy is for an applicant, when choosing between multiple admissions offers, to choose the second or third most rigorous school, one somewhat less competitive than the most rigorous option, to help ensure that the student will remain within the top third of his/her class at the school of choice. This is a late phase strategy that is less helpful in the school selection phase but effective after acceptances have come in and the time for the final decision of which school to take has arrived.

HIT PAUSE

At some point in the application process, the student or the parents may determine that the student is not ready to move on to boarding school. Hitting pause delays the process until the next year's admission cycle. There is no loss here; all of the effort and information can be applied, and likely be better applied, in the next go-round.

KEEPING OPTIONS OPEN

Not setting a specific strategy is a strategy in itself. There are many variables in boarding school admissions, too many to calculate. Financial aid is highly uncertain – one school may offer nothing, another huge amounts. An applicant's test scores may improve dramatically in the course of the admissions process. Families able to live with a high degree of uncertainty may decide to keep all options open right through the admissions cycle, apply to many types of schools, wait to see what happens, and then make choices from what results.

SOURCES OF INFORMATION

There are three sources for details about individual schools. The first is publications and online sites. The second is personal contact – with school representatives, alumni and parents. The third is in person visits to the schools themselves.

PUBLICATIONS

Peterson's Guide to Private Schools an encyclopedic reference of both day and boarding schools, is available at bookstores and libraries.

Note: Libraries tend to stock Peterson's Guides which are several years out of date. You will need the latest annual version to keep abreast of school statistics. Two other classic prep school catalogues that remain in some libraries, Porter Sargent's *Handbook of Private Schools* and *The Greenes' Guide to Boarding Schools*, are no longer published.

School brochures and catalogues are an engaging way to begin your search. Most schools offer beautiful, colorful brochures with wonderful photos of happy, healthy students. Catalogues will give you some data about the school, perhaps a campus map, some information about campus life, classes, and how to apply. *Student handbooks* reveal much about codes of conduct, disciplinary procedures, how schools deal with misbehavior, and an array of other issues. *Course catalogues* reveal the scope of the curriculum plus course and graduation requirements.

ONLINE

School Websites usually have links to school publications, videos, and school data. There might be photo or video tours of the campus, quick video interviews with students and faculty, news of school events and programs, and an admission portal with pages about tuition costs and financial aid.

Outside websites and blogs can be useful though their information can range widely in veracity and objectivity. Data posted tends to lag a year or two behind current numbers.

One reliable resource is *boardingschools.com*, the official site of TABS – The Association of Boarding Schools. Here you will find a wide array of information about boarding schools of all kinds plus useful essays, links, and resource information. *Boardingschoolreview.com* is a widely used information site with over three hundred boarding schools listed, with most in the US, some in Canada, and a few from the UK and Europe. This site has search tools that allow you to focus on schools by various metrics and tools that allow you to bookmark schools for comparative statistical analysis.

Various **private school organizations** provide information and assistance.

NAIS – National Association of Independent Schools

TABS – The Association of Boarding Schools

TSAO – Ten Schools Admissions Organization (Andover, Choate, Deerfield, Exeter, Hill, Hotchkiss, Lawrenceville, Loomis Chaffee, St. Paul's, Taft). TSAO is an admission consortium which produces a series of information events in US cities as well as internationally. These events allow families to investigate one, some, or all ten schools at one location. AOs are on hand to discuss their schools, answer questions, and distribute admission materials.

ESA - Eight Schools Association (Andover, Choate, Deerfield, Exeter, Hotchkiss, Lawrenceville, Northfield Mount Hermon, St. Paul's). ESA is a curriculum incubator and market research/strategy cooperative.

See Appendix A-Resources

PERSONAL CONTACT

Many schools send out their AOs on *regional tours* to major cities both in the US and internationally. Schools may schedule their own events or multi-school fairs in coordination with organizations such as TSAO or TABS.

Usually there's a formal presentation where the AOs give a short speech pitching their schools accompanied by plenty of brochures and catalogues. Finally, there's an informal meet and greet with snacks and drinks. It's a chance to chat, introduce yourself, and begin a personal relationship with the schools that interest you.

These events are always worth attending, whether or not you have already attended one. The prime reason is the chance to connect with the AOs. The more the AOs get to know a student, the more likely it is that they will act as an advocate when the admission committee meets. AOs are assigned by region, so most likely they will be coming back again within the same annual cycle.

Students should consider interviews with the AOs at these touring regional events. There are several advantages to this strategy. First, you are on your home turf, which can help your confidence level. Second, you are not on the school's campus, which can be intimidating amidst the crush of applicants waiting to interview during their campus tours. Best of all, if you interview at one of these events, probably not many others will be interviewing there, so you are more likely to capture the AO's complete attention.

Alumni, parents, and current students can be quite helpful to get up-to-date campus information that the websites don't have yet. Each can provide different types of information and opinions, none of which will be objective. Alumni info tends towards the nostalgic (how it was back in their student days) or the political – what's going on with the trustees or the administration. Parents have their eye on student support services and academics. Students can tell you about dorm life, the social scene, and all about the food service.

IN PERSON

The best source of all is visiting the schools. Your experience walking around a campus, sitting in on classes, visiting the dorms, talking with the students and the faculty will tell you more about a school than any catalogue, website or school fair ever can.

YOUR FIRST SCHOOL LIST

You have gathered information and looked at websites and catalogues. Now is the time to make your first list of schools. At this early stage, this list might be very long, but don't worry about that. You can always trim it down later. This list should include schools that can fulfill the student's needs and possibly some wants as well.

Try to keep an open mind and consider all sorts of options that would satisfy your needs and speak to your wants. If you lack experience in judging one type from another, include large schools and small, and perhaps both coed and single sex.

Put schools on this first list that interest or energize you. In "Comments" try to state why in particular. Sometimes, the quality at one school that appeals to you might be found at another.

As you and your family move along and learn more, your minds may change about what you want. This is natural and to be expected.

SCHOOL LIST #1

SCHOOL	NEEDS	WANTS	COMMENTS
1.			
2.			
3.			
4.			
5.			

SCHOOL	NEEDS	WANTS	COMMENTS
6.			
7.			
8.			
9.			
10.			

THE IMPORTANCE OF "FIT"

Schools are like shoes – one size does not fit all. Some schools are very difficult to get into, while others have more open admissions policies. Some have high stress academics, some are more relaxed. Some have friendly, inspiring campus cultures, others are rather cold and stern. In addition, individual students have different needs and wants, as do their families. One fantastic school may be much more suitable than another fantastic school, according to these differences.

Part of "fit" is an academic environment that will challenge your student more than the current school does but not so harshly as to be overwhelming. Some students at or near the top of their classes may enter a rigorous boarding school only to find themselves in the middle or lower third of the pack. This can be discouraging, but with hard work and better study skills, many make improvements and return to excellent academic performance.

Others in similar circumstances fare less well, lose heart and end up either with a poor academic record or dropping out entirely. This reaction can occur even with students with outstanding academic records, achievers who, for the first time in their lives, discover themselves less capable than many of their fellow students. This sudden loss of status can severely affect the new student's academic success, together with attendant medical, emotional and psychological problems. The affected student has not lost any intelligence or academic skill but compared to others feels suddenly deficient and insignificant. This circumstance is known as **relative deprivation**. Several reports target relative deprivation as the cause for widespread depression and other psychological issues among students at Ivy League and other elite universities.

CHAPTER 6
PHASE THREE - ZEROING IN

In Phase Two of your search, you gathered an initial list of schools for further investigation.

You may have a list of ten, twenty, or thirty possible schools. These numbers are too big to manage as actual applications, never mind the cost of all those application fees.

Now in Phase Three, the task is to draw down this list to a manageable number of schools, schools that are real candidates for application – **schools where your student, if admitted, can succeed and would enjoy attending.** The last phrase contains the three keys of your school search: admission – success – enjoyment. Together, these are called "fit".

Besides such concerns, academic fit can impact college admissions outcomes. The consequences can be posed as a question: which is a better situation for a student – to be in the bottom third of a class at an elite school or in the top third at a less rigorous school? The latter is the stronger option, with more opportunities for academic awards and school leadership positions plus higher esteem and less stress as well.

USING SSAT SCORES FOR ACADEMIC FIT

One approach to finding an academic "fit" is to compare the student's SSAT scores to the average SSAT scores at the schools that interest you. If the student's average sits at or above the school's average, you have a reasonable expectation that the student will adjust well to the new prep environment. If the student scores well above the average, there is increased likelihood of success. If the student scores well below, there is increase likelihood that the student will struggle.

Given this, it is advisable to aim for schools where the student's SSAT scores match or surpass the schools' SSAT average. It should be noted, however, that SSAT scores as an aspect of admissions have only limited value. Schools with average scores of 80 will be looking for scores around or above that score, but a student average of 90 does not mean automatic admission. SSAT scores should be considered as a barrier to pass through – once a student shows a strong score, the admissions office will turn to other aspects of the student's application.
So should you.

If the student has not taken the SSAT under real test conditions, take steps to schedule a test. If you are in the spring or summer months, you can schedule an unofficial test with a test center. (An official SSAT test in the spring or summer months will not be accepted by schools which want SSAT scores from tests administered during the next academic year.)

The SSAT Upper Level exam is for grades nine and up. (If the student is applying for 11th-12th grade, the school may ask for the PSAT, SAT, or ACT.) It consists of two Quantitative (math) sections of 30 minutes each, a Reading section (40 minutes) and a Verbal section (30 minutes). An ungraded writing sample (25 minutes) is an add-on. With breaks in between sections, the test runs about 155 minutes.

The point of taking an SSAT under test conditions is threefold: for practice, to observe any test score progress from earlier practice tests, and to give you some sense of admission prospects. If the student's SSAT scores have consistently been at the high end of the range, 90 and above, you can be assured that score outcomes for official SSAT exams will be similar. If the student's scores began rather low but have improved, it is likely that scores will improve some more. If there has been no overall rise in test scores, you should assume that the student's final SSAT scores will be within the current range.

REASSESSING YOUR SCHOOL LIST

Review the schools on your first list. Now that you have done some research, some schools may appear more likely candidates than others. Create a second school list with those standout schools.

Look up their admission rates: go to boardingschoolreview.com for school statistics. (Note: data on this site tends to be a year or two behind, but that's close enough, the admit rates don't vary widely year to year but do trend lower incrementally.)

Understand that overall admit rates actually disguise the real admit rates, because "hooked" applicants have much higher admit rates. Take a school with what appears to be a middle range admission rate, say 50%. On the face of it, five out of ten applicants are admitted, but let's look more closely. Some of those admits are legacies, they get preference. Some of them are athletes, also preferred. Add up all the hooked applicants and this may come to half or more. That's twenty five percent because half of the admitted students are pre-selected. Unhooked applicants are competing with each other to get in, not at a rate of two out of four, but a rate of one out of four! And that's a school with a 50% admit rate! When you consider a school with a 20% admit rate – well, we are talking about a very low statistical probability of admission.

USEFUL DATA DETAILS

The overall admit rate may be of interest, but more important are the numbers relating to you and the class you seek to enter:

ADMIT RATE BY GRADE

Keep in mind that the student is not competing for a place in general; there are only so many spots open per grade level. Some schools have more openings at certain grade levels.

BOARDING/DAY ADMIT RATES

The admission rate of boarding students versus day students at a school can vary widely from school to school, even those with similar overall admit rates. In some schools there is a much lower admit rate for day students, which skews the overall admit rate, disguising a more favorable boarding admit rate. In others, the opposite applies.

ACCEPTANCE RATE

A more difficult statistic to discover is the acceptance rate, the percentage of admitted students who accept a place and enroll. This is of real importance if the applicant lands on the wait list.

COLLEGE MATRICULATION

All prep schools proudly list the colleges where their recent graduates are now enrolled. Be skeptical of these numbers, not of their veracity, but what they signify. The fact that many students head to Yale does not mean that yours will, or that the school itself had much to do with this success. The fortunate Yalies might be great athletes or multi generational legacies; they might be the progeny of Hollywood celebrities or the spawn of high wealth parents willing to drop several million dollars to fund a new building. Equally, some prep school grads, eyeing the future costs of medical school or law school, eschew costly elite colleges for undergraduate study, opting instead for generous merit aid at less exalted state universities.

AP COURSES

Some families demand schools that offer Advanced Placement courses to prepare students for AP exams. This can be an important concern in public schools and in some day schools but not so much at boarding schools.

Advanced Placement courses and testing began as a project in 1951 between three boarding schools, Phillips Andover, Phillips Exeter and Lawrenceville and three colleges, Harvard, Princeton, and Yale. The objective was to create high school level courses specifically designed to prepare students for college level work. AP courses are now offered in many types of schools.

Over time, AP courses tended to focus on the AP final exam to the extent that they were derided as "teaching to the test", providing information but not substantial education. Now none of the three original AP boarding schools offer AP courses; these schools and many others assume that their regular course offerings are sufficient as preparation for AP exams and encourage their students to take the AP exams in the spring term. Consistently excellent test results bear out this decision.

FACULTY MORALE

This is a difficult aspect for outsiders to detect but discussion with faculty on campus can sometimes reveal discontents, however circumspect and positive teachers may appear. Unusual numbers of faculty resigning or retiring at a school should be considered as potential leading indicators of leadership trouble ahead.

ATHLETIC OPPORTUNITIES

Athletes will want to know more about a school's team dynamics going into the admissions process. High success teams, teams that have won championships, tend to be overloaded with graduating seniors and PGs – this may mean that that team is looking to replenish their rosters, an opportunity for entering students. Other schools may have teams that are on the rise, with 10th and 11th graders coming up and with less need for new players.

Athletes are advised to contact coaches well in advance of the normal application schedule; eighteen months ahead of your planned start at the school is not too early. Prep coaches usually are also teachers and can also be residential supervisors; it may take a while to get their attention. Start now with an email inquiry. Plan on sending some game highlight tapes. If you plan a campus tour, do everything you can to arrange to meet the coach.

EXTRACURRICULAR ACTIVITY OPPORTUNITIES

Schools can range widely in the programs they offer. Many have more advanced facilities and resources than others, with dedicated teachers and staff. Most likely, you will not be choosing schools because of their ECs, but the quality and variety of ECs could tip your decision to one school and away from another.

STUDENTS - DO SOME SLEUTHING

You can learn quite a lot about what's going on at boarding schools from social media. Most schools and student organizations have official Facebook accounts, many also use Instagram. Another good source is the student newspaper, often accessible online. Following prep students on Snapchat, Instagram and Twitter can tell you quite a lot that the school brochures don't mention (and sometimes don't want you to know).

THE CAMPUS TOUR

Now is a good point to discuss the matter of that classic boarding school tradition, the campus tour. The tour typically is thought of as part of the formal application process. In fact, the campus tour is not part of the application, because it is not required by the schools but it merits discussion as it has multiple uses.

The tour is very valuable as an opportunity for the student to meet, or meet again, with the admission officers. One way or another, the applicant needs to make a personal impression on the admission staff. The student who interviews off campus may be assigned a volunteer, such as an alumnus/alumna or a parent. That may be pleasant and positive but it is not sufficient. The AOs are pros, and they know how to engage and evaluate student applicants; volunteers lacking experience and training may or may not be as effective, nor will their recommendations likely carry as much weight as those from admission staffers.

A campus visit by the student and the family can make a lasting impression and demonstrates interest in the school. Students also may interview during the campus visit; most schools will schedule an interview ahead of the formal application, which typically is due in January (check each school for its particular application schedule deadlines). There is no requirement to interview during a campus visit, but it certainly saves time as opposed to scheduling a separate interview off campus or a second visit on campus to interview later.

Visiting a campus is an effective way to get a first real glimpse of the school, its community of students and teachers, and its culture. Walking around a school can give the student a much more vivid sense of what it might be like to go there than flipping through a school catalogue. The school's personality and the surrounding locale – the town and townspeople, the weather – suddenly become real. This too is an aspect of "fit", an unspoken feeling that draws (or repels) an applicant to a particular school. After campus tours, your list of schools can quickly come into clearer focus.

When to go? Some would argue that the summer months work best, to avoid the big crowds of applicants and their families that come during the fall months. Summer tours also don't eat into your student's fall school schedule. The big flaw in this approach is that boarding schools are very quiet in the summer. Without the regular students and faculty, it's impossible to gauge the true pulse of the school. What you are left with is a tour of the buildings and grounds plus perhaps some short summer programs, if the school has them, which are usually populated by visiting students from other schools – not what you need to see. Schedule a fall visit in harmony with other school tours and present school schedules. Many school admissions offices are closed in the summer months; they resume taking tour reservations after the fall term begins. Schedule your interviews as soon as possible to get the best deals on flights and accommodations. Don't delay, as tour reservations can quickly "sell out" for the entire fall term. Try to schedule for early fall, ahead of proceeding with applications. Late fall tour dates can conflict with your student's current school exams and schedules. Group schools geographically. Plan for two per day at most.

You must check with each school you wish to visit to book a tour. Not all days are available for tours. If possible, schedule visits on weekdays to avoid crowds (and boy, are there crowds!) This may require your student to miss quite a few days of school, and school work may suffer as a consequence. Current sports coaches won't be happy either. Some teachers may help by giving out homework in advance so the student can work on the plane or on the drive to the schools and in the hotels. This is actually good practice. Boarding school students often have to do homework whenever and wherever they can grab time – in a hall between classes, on a campus lawn, or on the field hockey bus coming back from a game.

Usually, the campus tour will not be the over-riding factor in the decision whether to apply or not – but on the other hand, it might be. If you get a personal tour with an AO, take this as a clear sign that the student is particularly interesting to the school. Usually, however, tours are conducted by student guides.

These students are chosen for their poise and charm. Sometimes, though, you don't get one of these, and even the most congenial kid is going to have a bad day once in a while. Keep in mind that this one student is not the school, and try not to judge the school based on one person.

This is difficult to do when the tour guide is the chief, perhaps the only, person from that school with whom you spend much time. The remedy for this folds neatly into the best tour advice I can give you: visit the people, not the place.

ADVICE FOR STUDENTS

Your trip to the school is not to walk around some buildings. You need to meet the community, the people that you may be living with. So meet them! Ahead of your visit, ask the admission office if you can meet students who are involved in the sorts of activities that you would want to do. Ask also to speak with faculty.

If the school has a formal dress code, dress to that code for campus visits and interviews. If this clothing style feels weird, practice wearing these clothes ahead of time.

On the tour day, get to campus early. Why? To get comfortable, to get acquainted with the place before you go to the admission office. Walk around, look around. If you know there's a facility or program on campus that interests you, check it out. Don't expect that the scheduled tour will include what you like – the guide may never get around to it! After your stroll, it's time to check in at admissions. Introduce yourself to every AO you meet, starting with the receptionist. Collect their business cards, chat, express yourself. If you are interviewing before the tour, you will already be more relaxed and likely more confident having had a few informal chats along your walk. If you have already interviewed, try to check in with the AO who interviewed you to say hello. If you plan to interview later, introduce yourself to the AOs anyway; make your presence felt.

If you manage to set up meetings with students and faculty, be ready to ask them core questions: How do they like the school? How long have they been there? How's the food? Just get a conversation going. If you can, get enthusiastic.

Typically, the scheduled tour is a not very interesting walk to look at one academic building after another. Be aware that schools are trying to "sell" you, and the tour of fabulous facilities is one way to do that. Try to focus on people – if you can get the tour guide's attention, try to connect one-on-one. This is difficult of course, as the guide is trying to manage a group of visitors. If there are other current students helping the guide, talk with them. If the tour is quick and students are not available, don't worry. Just go with the flow. There will be opportunities later to engage current students.

One very important place on a scheduled tour is the dorm. You need to check out the living quarters, and many schools don't allow visitors in the dorms except on the tours. You should assume that the dorm you are touring is the best one, the newest one, the one with the largest rooms or best facilities, and the one that has been cleaned and neatened up well beyond the everyday.

As you walk around the campus, try to concentrate on the facilities that you will actually use, not just the buildings that are impressive architecture.

Places to study: Does the school provide plentiful areas to study outside of the dorm rooms? This is a basic survival requirement; studying in your room all the time can drive you crazy. Also, given the intense daily scheduling, you may find you need to grab half an hour or forty-five minutes to finish some assignment but walking back to your room is out of the question. This is a big issue on many campuses, yet incredibly, more than a few schools don't have many places for students to study outside of their rooms or the library, which usually is totally booked up anyway.

Places to congregate: Boarding school students need places to hang out and socialize. Besides the dorms, where do you go? Again, some schools overlook this critical aspect. Social interaction isn't incidental to the boarding experience; it's actually as important as the academics. These spaces need not be consciously dedicated to student socializing, they can just be informal areas. You can hang out on the lawns and porches in the warm months, but in the winter, you don't want to spend all of your free time in your room.

Athletic facilities are critical to some sports, not so much to others. Areas to look into include training facilities, sports medicine and physical therapy resources, and technology resources.

Activity centered areas: If you make films, are there post production facilities? If you are into television, is there a sound stage? If you play an instrument, are practice rooms plentiful? If you are into painting or sculpture, how are the studio spaces?

Students: Once the tour is done, thank your guide and ask for an email for any more questions you might have. Return to the admissions office to personally thank the staff. Get their emails as well for follow-up correspondence.

Remember, all of this – for you – is to make an agreeable impression that sticks. Stay on campus a bit longer, maybe even walk around on your own if you feel okay with that. How does the school feel? Is this a place that seems interesting? As soon as you can, sit down somewhere and record your notes about what you feel and think – the pros and cons of that school, that community. Write them down or have your family film you with a cell phone as you talk about your reactions to the school. Do this right away, before you move on to another school. Sometimes while thinking through your impressions, you will remember something you forgot to ask or think of a new question for the AOs or the students. As you are still at the school, you can go back and get the answer you want. Once you leave for the airport or drive to the next school to tour, this opportunity will be lost.

Follow up with handwritten thank-you cards or letters sent to the Dean of Admission and every AO you met. If possible, do this the same day you take your tour – say in the hotel that evening. If that is not practical, write and mail these thank-you notes as soon as possible on your return home. Time is critical – if you procrastinate, you may forget who was who and what you said and thought about that school.

Campus tours sometimes prompt students to cross some schools off of their lists – something about the school or the surrounding community is a major turnoff. Others get excited about schools they were not really wild about. Still others find that the tour reinforces their original thoughts. Any way it works out, you can be assured that a campus tour is worth the time, expense, and effort – you will have a stronger sense of the school and whether you want to apply or not.

If your tour is exciting, you might consider returning to that school again in another season, during a regular school week.

You will learn more about the school and meet more people, and a return visit demonstrates your real interest in the school. Second visits by applicants are not typical; AOs will notice and take note.

On the opposite end of the spectrum are families that cannot visit schools at all and must rely on internet materials, phone calls, and off campus interviews. Such circumstances typically arise for international families and also for families lacking the financial wherewithal to travel at this stage of the process. If this is your situation, do not fret. Initial school tours are not required by the schools. What's more, it is entirely possible that you will not receive an acceptance from schools that you have toured. Alternatively, you can always tour a school once you have received an acceptance – this is called a "revisit". Most families return for revisits to the schools that have offer acceptances in order to make their final decision. If you have only one opportunity to visit a school, choose the revisit, after you have received an offer of admission.

INTERVIEW WITH THE TOUR?

Typically, prospective students and their families visit a campus for an interview and a tour. As the interview is one of the most critical aspects of your admissions application, it makes sense to think carefully about the terms and circumstances of your interview.

Some schools will schedule the interview first with a tour to follow. This can be tough on the student. Starting off with a critical aspect of an application on a strange campus, often at the start of the day, can be a less than ideal situation. You might ask to tour first and interview afterwards. Walking around on a tour will help the student wake up (if it is morning) and help calm any jitters. Chatting with student guides and passing students can make the student feel more comfortable on campus. By the time the tour ends back at the admissions office, the student will likely feel more confident.

If the tour goes well, the student will know more about the school and may be more energized and excited about applying to it. This enthusiasm can carry over into the interview, a decided plus. If the tour is a turn off, the student might want to leave immediately; instead, stick with the schedule and have the student interview anyway. This is great practice, you're there anyway, and you never know – that school may look better a few months down the line.

The interview is a major part of the application and will be discussed in more detail in the following chapter on the application process.

SECOND SCHOOL LIST

During the fall term, you will need to narrow down your list of schools. Read over your first list and the notes you made about what interested you about each. Some schools may seem less interesting now, others more. Parents may lean one way, the student may another – keep an open mind, opinions changes and so do family circumstances.

Make a new list of schools that continue to interest you and possibly new ones not on the first list. Your list will change because you – all of you – are changing. Again, list your reasons why each school is attractive. This is not a trivial exercise. You will need to refer to this list and the reasons later in this process.

HOW MANY SCHOOLS?

Is there a recommended number of schools to which to apply? As family situations vary widely, there is no fixed number, but there is an upper limit – that limit is however many applications you can manage in the time you have until the applications deadlines. This is usually four months – September to January, when many school applications are due. Some school application deadlines extend until the end of January, with some later than that; some schools have rolling admissions with no fixed deadlines. You probably can't get a head start on the September beginning point, because online school admission portals do not open up until the start of the school year and the essay prompts (the essay questions or subjects) often change annually. If you write an essay using last year's essay prompt, you may find that you will have to write another one when the new prompts are posted. This keeps your application writing window between September and January. If you can handle five applications, and you would love to go to one of five specific schools, apply to those five schools. If you can handle eight, and love those eight, apply to eight. One variation is to choose your top group – perhaps two to four – and plan to get all of those applications prepared carefully. Have a second list of schools, again two to four. These applications you will complete only if time allows.

Some families apply to many schools, twelve or more, calculating that this increases the odds for admission, but applying only to schools with low acceptance rates may not result in multiple offers. A downside of applying to many schools is a loss in student intensity for the individual schools. Boarding schools are looking for passionate applicants, those who truly want to attend that particular school. Is it possible to be passionate for every one of 12-15 schools?

On the other hand, you should also consider a lower limit. Be aware that opinions may shift a lot during the application process. If you are targeting only one school or two or three, there may come a point when none of this small number is really a good "fit". The "dream" school sometimes turns out not to seem so dreamy; the student's perspective on what schools to aim for can suddenly shift radically midway through the quest and sometimes even at the last moment. Also the family's needs may shift during the search process, requiring school options other than the few on the list.

PART III -
ALL ABOUT ADMISSION

At this next stage in your journey, parents and students take on separate responsibilities.

The application itself is and should be chiefly the task of the student, to whom Chapter 7 is addressed.

Aspects of financing a boarding school education are concerns for the parent, to whom Chapter 8 is addressed.

Both students and parents must understand admission deadlines and decisions, discussed in Chapter 9.

CHAPTER 7
THE APPLICATION PROCESS

Your school quest now shifts into Phase #4 of the admission process: completing formal applications. This phase is not just a series of tasks; it is also a transition. In the early stages of this journey, the parent may have been the prime motivator. Now in the application stage, the student must step up to the main role with the parent providing support.

The application process is deadline driven and complex: each school has its own application details and procedures. To navigate this phase successfully, keep your deadline(s) in mind. January 15 is the application deadline for many schools, some use January 30, and some have rolling deadlines. Don't get these mixed up, and don't wait until the last month to write essays. Some schools can be flexible if a deadline is missed. Others have drop-dead deadlines with no flexibility.

Keep a separate checklist for each school. Triple-check whether each required document has been uploaded or mailed. Application enclosures that must be obtained from other people can take much longer than you ever imagined. You should expect that they WILL take much longer. The single biggest challenge is student essays; the single biggest headache – teacher recommendations (discussed later).

It pays to go to the website of every school on the short list and carefully review the application information in the admission section of each site. Schools have similar guidelines for many aspects of the application but radically different rules for others. **Additional applicant materials** is one area that varies from school to school. For example, some schools accept video materials in DVD form, others require a YouTube link, while others accept none. Some schools accept photos and artwork support materials uploaded in pdf files only, others allow or require other means and formats and procedures.

USING COMMON APPLICATIONS

Efforts have been made to simplify the application procedure with common application portals that can be used for multiple school applications. These attempts have had some success:

The Enrollment Management Association, which offers the SSAT, maintains its own common application, the Standard Application Online or SAO (www.ssat.org)

Gateway to Prep Schools also has a common application (www.gatewaytoprepschools.com) for many popular boarding schools.

These online systems require you to create a user account and password. You can work on your application as time allows, logging in and out. The systems store your work as you progress. You can select which schools receive the applications. This information is confidential; if you apply to more than one school in a common application system, the schools do not know where else you may be applying. The sites charge an administrative fee for each school applied to through the site.

The Association of Boarding Schools (TABS) also has a common application. Its great asset is that it can be used for over two hundred schools (www.boardingschools.com). Its big downside is that it has no online portal. You must download the TABS common application in PDF, print it and fill out the hard copy.

Though all three common applications have numerous schools in their systems, none of these systems have all boarding schools on them. A number of schools are on only one of them, and some schools are on none of them at all.

This may result in quite different outcomes, depending on the schools on your list. You might find all of your schools on one of these common application sites, one or two on each site, or end up applying to each school from the individual school sites.

However it works for you, take the effort to visit the admission pages of each of the schools on your list. Oftentimes, the schools post critical information, such as details of what they are looking for in an application or in an applicant - information that a common application won't give you.

APPLICATION STRATEGY

Admission is often a scary prospect for students who hope they are admitted to the schools they love. Let's try to turn all this around. Admission shouldn't be scary. You have a lot to offer. You just need to present yourself well enough that the schools can see your potential.

At base, each school is asking two fundamental questions: "Who are you?" and "Why should we take you?" Your application must answer these two questions convincingly: "Who are you?" is one of the great questions in life, asked of everyone from Oedipus to Alice in Wonderland. It's not easy to answer or to explain, especially for a young person barely out of childhood. Somehow, though, you need to present yourself – through your interview, your essays, your academic record and your activities.

Presenting yourself well is critical, but not enough; you must also respond to the second question, "Why should we take you?" To answer strongly, you need to understand the school – its assets, its personality, its culture – and clearly explain why you want to go there. Perhaps that school has sports you play; perhaps the school's traditions or campus atmosphere attract you. There might be programs you want to explore or certain clubs you want to join. Remember those notes you took when you wrote your school lists? They come into play now. What aspects of this particular school attracted you to it in the first place? What can you contribute to that school's community?

Some applicants have obvious answers to these questions, as they may already be pursuing their talents at a high level as top scholars, athletes, or artists. They have plenty of past success to be proud of. If you don't happen to have a lot of achievements to crow about, don't be discouraged (and don't apologize). Set your imagination and passions to work on envisioning your future – what projects and goals you are aiming for, and what you hope to contribute while at the school.

You may be applying to several schools with a scattergun approach, hoping somehow you will get into one of them. If you keep thinking that way, you may well not get into any. The admissions people are focused on their school. It's the only one they care about and they can tell right away if you have real interest in their school or not. This is a big reason why "prestige" is a terrible motivation to apply to a school. It's like telling someone you want to be her friend because she lives in the right zip code.

Your application needs to be coherent. Every part needs to support the whole, and no part should repeat information cited in another part. Relying on volume – a clutter of random achievements, hobbies, and interests - won't help your case.

Whether you emphasize past success or future plans, your application isn't a plea, begging the school to admit you. You aren't asking them to make a decision. You are making an offer – all they have to do is say yes. If saying yes is easier than saying no, they will say yes.

STANDARD APPLICATION COMPONENTS
APPLICANT PROFILE (aka Student Questionnaire)

This section gathers the basics: name, age, contact information, school attendance history, whether applying as a boarding or day student, applying for financial aid, legacy status. Schools also want to know the applicant's ethnicity, native language, country of birth and country of citizenship, and visa/passport information. These aspects affect admission. If English is a second language, a TOEFL (English fluency test) may be required. Financial aid tends to flow to American citizens and residents. International citizenship or residence has admission value as schools like wide geographic representation. The applicant's educational history, legacy status (if any), grade level and proposed grade level entering the school are important.

If you are using a professional admissions advisor, you must declare this and provide information – name, contact data, and professional affiliations. This information allows the advisor to submit components of the application on the student's behalf and also alerts the school that the applicant is benefitting from professional guidance.

FAMILY PROFILE

This section gathers information regarding the status of parents and caregivers – biological parents, divorce or separation, who has legal custody and who will be financially responsible for the student's education. Schools want to know the parents' educational background, occupations, and job titles plus siblings' school and college education. This information gives the schools some idea of the applicant family's financial and educational resources.

Note: each school charges an **application fee**. Financial Aid applicants can request a fee waiver (see the next chapter for detailed information on Financial Aid)

TEACHER RECOMMENDATIONS

Most prep school applications require recommendations from the applicant's current English and Math teachers. The forms for these recommendations ask the teacher to comment on the applicant's academic achievement and potential, work habits, personality, character, and reputation among teachers and fellow students. The forms are typically filed directly by the teachers to the schools (you provide stamped, addressed envelopes) or through the common application online service portal, so that these commentaries are confidential. The student never sees them. The student must make arrangements for the teachers to fill out these forms in time to submit them by the application(s) deadlines.

As simple as this may seem, gathering teacher rec letters can be nightmarish for some. Here's why: the schools want recommendations from your English and Math teachers, whether you happen to excel in these subjects or you are just awful in them. You cannot substitute other instructors, they want rec letters from your English and Math teachers – period. Just as nerve-wracking, the schools expect letters from current English and Math teachers, whether or not you get along well with those teachers. You may have had wonderful, truly supportive Math and English teachers last year, but sorry, the schools want this year's teachers. Plus, the latest you can possibly get these rec letters is by the end of the winter break or a few weeks after (take this advice – don't wait that long, the stress is murder). So, in other words, you need rec letters from teachers who hardly know you!

Steady yourself, there are remedies:

1. Take extra care to work hard in those two courses and make a real effort to gain your teacher's support and approval well before you ask them for rec letters.

2. Ask the teachers early enough that they have time to write the letters but not so early that they know nothing about you. A sweet spot for this in October, after you have had a full half of the fall term (and possibly a midterm exam or project) but before the holiday season starts up.

3. Try to arrange for a meeting with each teacher so you can explain your plans for boarding school - why you are applying, what you hope to gain. If the teacher agrees to meet, bring an **information packet**. If you can't get a face-to-face meeting with the teacher, write a letter explaining your plans and deliver it with the info packet for the teacher's later review.

This packet should include:

A letter thanking the teacher for writing the recommendation (be sure to include the deadline for the rec letter!)

A summary (1-2 pages) of your academic, athletic, and activity achievements plus pertinent biographical information – family background, your interests, travels, or goals. Don't expect them to know much about you – give them some upbeat, interesting info to discuss! This is particularly important if you don't happen to be doing all that well in that English or Math class.

The recommendation form plus instructions on how to submit/file, brochures, catalogue, materials from some of the schools.

Remember that the number of schools has an impact here – the teacher may or may not be able to use the body of one rec letter for all school rec forms. If you are applying to a lot of schools, you can cut down the recommender's task somewhat by using a common application for at least some of the schools.

Boarding school is an entirely foreign concept to many teachers, especially public school teachers. Some may be hostile to boarding schools and/or resent that the student is leaving the current school. The applicant can counter any negative reactions by explaining (in person or in a letter) why this opportunity is so important and how difficult it is to gain admission and expressing gratitude for the teacher's help.

Another common challenge is teacher procrastination. Teachers are usually overworked as it is and you are asking them for a significant favor that offers zero benefit to them. Managing to persuade teachers to write strong rec letters before the deadline, without annoying them, is no easy task. On one hand, it makes sense to ask the teacher well into the fall term, after the applicant can establish a strong class record and make friends with the teachers. On the other, the teachers' workloads pile up as the term moves towards final exams.

Be patient but gently persistent. Try to get the teachers to submit and send their letters ahead of fall term's finals. If this fails, reset the deadline for sometime during the winter break. If that fails, reset it for the resumption of school in early January. If all else fails, find an alternative recommender (for example, a current History or Journalism teacher to replace an English teacher, or a science teacher to replace the math teacher), then call each boarding school to propose this substitute plan; you will need approval ahead of such a major switch.

EXTRACURRICULAR RECOMMENDATION

Some schools ask for an extracurricular recommendation from an adult who coaches, teaches or guides the applicant in a nonacademic activity. This is an excellent opportunity for the applicant to stand out from the crowd. Choose a recommender from one of your core activities. If a school does not require this additional recommendation, ask if one would be allowed.

PRINCIPAL RECOMMENDATION AND SCHOOL REPORT

Many schools also want a recommendation and School Report from the head of the current school. If the school is large and/or the head is not familiar with the applicant, an appropriate school official can substitute, e.g., if the applicant is enrolled in the current school's IB program, the IB director could complete the recommendation and School Report.

The School Report provides information about the current school – how it grades, whether it ranks students, the student population, etc – and about the applicant – is the applicant in good standing? The Report will also list the student's number of absences, tardies, disciplinary action, and/or withdrawals. The School Report is not confidential, and you should make it a point to look at it before it is sent off to the schools. If there is anything unusual in it, be prepared to provide an explanation if asked during admission interviews.

ADDITIONAL RECOMMENDATION

Some schools will allow an additional recommendation outside of the required ones. Some applicants pounce on this in hopes of bulking up their candidacies. This tactic is rarely of any value. Many school admissions offices have no time to read them; some forbid them entirely. If you happen to have an insider connection to a particular school – a supportive school administrator, trustee, or teacher – they will likely make a call on your behalf; a formal letter from such a connection is not necessary. Anything beyond this – testimonials from local dignitaries, relatives, or family friends – is rarely effective and just clutters up your application file.

TRANSCRIPTS

The applicant's transcripts for the most recent full marking period and the past full year must be sent to the boarding school directly from the current school. Transcripts usually require a small fee paid to the current school. More than one school may need to send transcripts if the applicant transferred schools recently. Most schools will not accept transcripts sent by the applicants or advisors.

The schools will be looking closely at your transcripts for the current school year and the year past. The details of your academic history before that will not be important. Admissions officers will note transcripts which show a consistent focus on challenging courses. An upward trend in grades is also a major plus. If your transcript reveals real crashes in core subjects, be prepared to explain poor grades, either in interviews or in application essays. Your peripheral elective courses will have less impact and consequence.

ENTRANCE TESTS

All prep schools, boarding and day, require applicants to take an entrance examination, as discussed earlier. Applicants applying to 9th or 10th grade usually take the SSAT or ISSE. (ISSE tends to be popular at western prep schools and at day schools.) Applicants for 11th grade may take the SSAT, ISEE PSAT, SAT or ACT. Applicants for 12th or PG grades take the PSAT, SAT or ACT.

SUBJECT PREP

Math sections are the simplest to prep for because specific areas of weakness can be identified and addressed. Take a practice test. Analyze your wrong answers and focus on those math areas with a tutor, or with Khan Academy, IXL, or other online resources. Test sections centered on vocabulary can be prepped for by studying word lists. There are vocabulary apps for the SAT and SSAT. Reading comprehension is the most difficult area to prep for quickly. Continued reading of literature, history, and similar subjects is advisable. Practice test questions centered on contextual information, comparisons, and conclusions can help.

TEST PREP AND SCHEDULING

Take your entrance exam soon after completing test preparations. Schools accept grades from multiple SSAT tests. Plan on taking the test twice. The test schedule begins in September, with exams scheduled each month after that. Schools usually will take test results through January. Take the first test no later than October. If you get excellent scores, above the averages for the schools to which you are applying, you're done with testing; turn to other aspects of your application. If your scores are not what you had hoped for, you have time to study more and then retest in December or January.

The SSAT charges a fee for each testing registration. Each test date has a regular registration period, then additional late and rush registration periods, each with additional fees. The domestic rate applies to test locations in all of the US, Canada, and some US territories. The international rate applies everywhere else. Families who cannot pay all or part of this fee may apply for a fee waiver. See ssat.org for more information.

SSAT scores are reported in the applicant's SSAT account; the scores are not automatically sent to the schools unless the applicant orders this ahead of the test. Applicants may direct SSAT to do this, but there is no advantage to doing so if the test results are not strong. Many applicants wait to see their scores before sending them to the schools or decide to retest in hopes of higher scores. After taking the test two or more times, the applicant can decide which tests to send to the schools.

Many schools use **superscoring** when considering multiple test scores. Superscoring takes the best scores from individual test sections, regardless of which test sitting they come from. Here is an example:

Applicant SSAT scores for the three section from testing #1: 550-720-680. From testing #2: 640-710-690. The superscore for these tests would be 640-720-690. Schools that do not superscore will take the best overall score from the scores submitted, in this case being 640-710-690. Applicants should ask each school about its superscoring policy.

When an applicant takes the SSAT two or more times, the schools are notified of multiple testing but are told not how many times. Schools do not know what other schools are receiving your SSAT scores (unless you tell them – they may ask).

TOEFL

A foreign applicant who speaks English as a second or third language will likely be asked by the school to take the Test of English as a Foreign Language (TOEFL). Requirements for fluency in English as well as school support and English as a Second Language programs (ESL) vary from school to school. International applicants should contact each school regarding their requirements and programs.

INDIVIDUALIZED APPLICATIONS COMPONENTS

Strong standard application components – grades, scores and recommendations – are important to a point. They help you get into the 'consider pile". Now your task is to find ways to set yourself apart from other applicants and make your case for admission. The individualized components – the interview, the essays, and the personal statement – are opportunities to show the admissions officers who you are as an individual, your interests, your enthusiasms, your sense of humor and way of thinking.

THE PERSONAL STATEMENT aka "ANYTHING ELSE?"

The Personal Statement is your strongest asset in your application. This is your opportunity to state why you are excited by the school, what you bring to the school community, and what goals you hope to achieve as a student there.

The Personal Statement is as important as your interview, maybe more important. If you rock your interview, the interviewer (preferably an AO) will be your strong advocate in the admission meetings. This is a tremendous asset, but that interviewer is only one person. No one else interviewed you, and in many cases, few or none of the other "deciders" on the admission team have even met you.

The Personal Statement is like an interview with the entire admissions department. It's on paper and every AO will get a copy – they all will read what you write. This has power. There is an old Latin saying, "verba volant, scripta manent": "The spoken word flies away, the written word remains."

There is one big danger with the Personal Statement – overlooking it in the application packet. Seriously. Gateway's common application and some individual school applications clearly indicate the Personal Statement as an important component of the application for admission, but amazingly, some application formats do not list the Personal Statement at all! Instead, there is a question that offers a chance for you to "say something more about yourself" or "is there anything else you would like us to know?" If you aren't paying attention, you could blow right by this without a second thought. Don't do that!

ESSAYS

At first glance, the Essay appears to be an opportunity to demonstrate your skill with written argument. Please set aside this assumption. No one cares how clever you are as a writer. What the admissions people want to know is how you express yourself, and deeper than that, who you are. An admission essay that really rocks shows a side of the student that can't be seen through a survey of grades, test scores, or recommendation letters. So show yourself, speak in your own "voice". Easier said than done: you are a young person. You're a work in progress.

Usually schools provide "prompts" – essay subjects or questions. There often are several prompts to choose from. This is a good thing; they can save you the trouble and stress of trying to figure out what to write about.

How do you choose a prompt? Your brilliant mind is already on display in your grades and test scores. Instead, pick a prompt that you connect with emotionally and write about that. Or one that strikes you as funny. Or creepy. Or sweet. Whatever you choose, write about something that you relate to and avoid sweeping generalities – teenagers pontificating about saving the planet or fighting homelessness tend to come off as pretentious. Instead, write about a friend, a family member, a dream you had, a trip you went on, something you learned, something that you remember – something that is real for you. This essay is not a class assignment. This is a story about you and what you want to say. Yes, check the grammar and spelling. Yes, write with clarity and concision, but write freely, without an imaginary teacher looming over you.

A few words of advice about parents. This is your major chance to show your true self. Parents should not micromanage the essay or even read it until you have worked it over for a while.

Parents best serve as copy editors, checking for errors, and also as objective readers, to give feedback as to whether or not the essay is clear.

One very important subject: do not cheat. More than a few applicants have been caught using someone else's essay as their own. Also understand that you can not write these essays ahead of time. Many schools will create new essay prompts each year which are available when the new admission packets are released in September. If you try to get your essays out of the way in the summer, you may well find that you have to write brand new essays come September. Then again, do not wait until January to begin writing them!

THE INTERVIEW

Interviews are absolutely critical for your candidacy.

The interview is your best chance to:

—demonstrate your enthusiasm for the particular school like no other part of your application

—show your willingness to engage, to participate in a conversation, and to hold your own in it with an adult

—and from all this, to grab the attention of the AO and turn him/her into your advocate in the admissions room.

So, no pressure, right?

HOW TO PREPARE FOR THE INTERVIEW

Plan on looking like you belong on that campus – wear clothes according to the school requirements. Check out the catalogue and website in advance. If you are applying to a "traditional" school, practice getting used to wearing such clothes ahead of the interview. You want to look like you fit in, but you also want to feel comfortable.

The interview isn't a test and there are no right or wrong answers. The critical part is to be yourself, and be enthusiastic about whatever truly gets you enthusiastic. Find something about that school that excites you and talk about that.

Typical prep interviews go something like this. Nervous kid and nervous parents meet the AO. There's a brief cordial chat. Then the AOs "invites" the parents to wait in the reception area outside. The parents leave. The kid sits in agony alone on the couch while the AO settles into a chair. Then silence. The AO tries to get something going with a generic question. "How was your trip?" "Have you had a chance to look around campus?" Most kids answer dutifully.

Then more silence. A few more generic questions. Then, ding! Time's up. Some people try to guess standard questions that interviewers will ask: What's your favorite book? Why do you want to come to this school? What did you do last summer? These are standard questions, and yes, interviewers may ask them if they have to. Interviews are scheduled tightly – assume ten minutes max per student – and time is ticking on. If the conversation isn't going anywhere, yes, the interviewer will ask some generic question just to get you talking.

Instead, think about what you want to talk about and start the conversation yourself. Talk about what excites you about the school, what programs you are interested in, and your thoughts about college and beyond. If you have some good questions for the AO, ask them. Don't ask questions just for the sake of asking questions. If you ask, "how many students do you have?" you are merely telling the AO that you didn't even bother to do any research on the school at all.

Instead ask questions you can't get from research or questions that came up today as you walked around campus.

There is one aspect that you can prep for – the circumstances of the interview. Attend some school tour events (AOs visiting your area) or boarding school fairs (check with TABS). If there aren't any near where you live, go to other events – college fairs, church groups, or any informational event where you can meet adults. Why? To practice introducing yourself and carrying on a conversation.

Your interviewing skills will improve as you go; try not to schedule your favorite school first.

Don't overthink how the interview goes. If it is short and without much connection, it does not necessarily cancel out your candidacy. (You can also request another interview.)

If it goes well and the AO is complimentary and upbeat – this is not an act. Take it as a good sign.

Maintain the relationship with a thank-you note, emails, and texts (avoid phone messages).

PARENT INTERVIEW

Schools usually interview the parents of legacy applicants as a matter of courtesy and often interview the parents of non legacy students. These interviews are usually separate from the student's and without the student's presence.

Parent interviews are brief and have limited objectives, chiefly to discover who is the prime motivator of the application and whether the parents support their student going away to school. Beyond these issues, your parents need not worry whether or not they impress the interviewer.

STUDENT QUESTIONNAIRE

Virtually all applications ask the student to list participation in school and non-school activities. Your log of activities discussed in Part II comes into play now.

List your school achievements with explanations and context: if you were on the Principal's Honor Roll, how many other students were on it out of a total school population of how many students? Cite any leadership positions you held and any awards or recognitions you received in academics, school clubs and athletics, student government, etc. Don't limit yourself to official activities. Did you do anything on your own – introduce any innovations, start a club, or organize some school events? Say so. What are your future school plans – what sports, clubs, and service plans? This list is not boasting – this is making your case for admission.

Then, non-school achievements – in volunteer groups, church, scouting, or athletics. Again, awards, honors, and recognition. Include your own projects, whatever your interests or work activities: robotics, cooking, camping, babysitting, or volunteering.

Some applications also ask you to describe your summer activities and books you have read recently. Again, add explanation and context. If you worked as a lifeguard, add something beyond "worked as lifeguard"; explain any training you did, your job responsibilities, any unusual or notable situations you were involved in, and what you gained and learned, etc.

Listing books read could include brief summaries of how a book affected you, changed your thinking, or motivated you to read other books.

PARENT STATEMENT

Some schools invite parents to write an essay about their student. This is always optional and completely voluntary. Some parents agonize over what to say and how to say it.

The advice here is: tell your parents to keep it short, simple and true and rein in any impulse to gush. They should write something about you that is not seen anywhere else in the application, something that only a parent can give, something touching or funny, an event or a memory.

STUDENTS - PLAY YOUR BEST CARD

The strongest aspect of your application is not your grades, your test scores, nor your recommendations. Your best asset is you – your character, your sense of humor, your insights, your unique personality. You might be an outgoing comedian; you might be fascinated by math; you might be shy and sensitive. However you are, be that – in the interview, in your essays, and when interviewing and talking with students on campus. These are all opportunities to express your true self – not what you think you think the school wants or what your parents want. You are unique, so be unique! Be you!

CHAPTER 8
FINANCES

American boarding schools are as famous for their costs as for the educations they provide. Many are as pricey as the priciest colleges, and costs keep rising.

Why is the cost of boarding school so high, especially compared to U.S. income? The answer to that question is made of several parts. First is the flatlining of most American incomes in the past several decades; costs keep rising, but overall domestic incomes have not kept up. Second is the devaluation of the American dollar. In 1964, $3,000 was the general going rate for annual prep tuition. In 2014, that would be equal to $22,626. So where does the other $44,000 of the current cost come from? Some of this derives from increased regulation and restrictions – these old schools often are under costly covenants, National Historic Register mandates, and insurance and legal requirements that affect many aspects of school management, from facilities maintenance and expansion to accounting requirements to safety and liability concerns. The schools have added many more programs, advanced facilities, and creature comforts for the students than existed in decades past. To manage all of these changes, the schools have added new layers of administrative personnel, another major cost addition.

COSTS

TUITION, ROOM & BOARD

Tuition, room & board are the major expenses of a boarding school education. In 2014, the median total expense (tuition, fees, and room & board) for grade 9-12 boarding schools in the United States was $66,036, according to the NAIS. As a comparison, Harvard tuition, fees, and room and board in 2014-2015 came to $58,607. The mean income in the United States for 2014 was $53,657.

At sixty six thousand dollars per year (more now), only the most well-off families can consider paying full tuition without making significant spending adjustments or seeking financial aid. Plus, tuition does not cover the total annual cost per student. Many schools report a cost gap of 20-30%, which must be made up by school support.

ADDITIONAL EXPENSES

There are other expenses that add to the overall expense.

Fees are school charges apart from tuition – technology fees, health service fees, and tuition insurance (covering the tuition should the student need to withdraw from the school). Some schools charge an international student fee. Families also need to factor in the fees paid during the school search and application processes: application fees, test fees, tutoring, and test prep fees.

Textbooks are costly, with some well over a hundred dollars each. Families can expect to pay another $1,000 for new textbooks and school supplies annually. Some savings can be had by renting textbooks or finding used ones. Mercifully, many schools are shifting to e-textbooks and online resources which help keep book costs down.

Other School Costs include medical charges (accident exams, x-rays, etc), athletic gear, activity supplies, and some course supplies – art and science classes sometimes have additional charges. Families that opt for laundry service may pay that charge at registration; charges vary widely from school to school.

"HIDDEN" COSTS

We are not done yet. There are other expenses which are "hidden" in a sense, because families tend to overlook them in the rush to admissions.

Travel – transportation to and from school can be a major expense, depending on where the school is and where the family is. Regular student travel is to be expected. These schools require students to leave campus during the major breaks – Thanksgiving, winter, spring, and summer. Unless the family makes other arrangements, this can mean four student roundtrip airfares plus airport shuttle service. Family travel can also add up as parents and possibly siblings travel to school for parent/teacher conferences on parents weekend, college counseling sessions during the winter, and possibly other trips or campus events. Student trips of various kinds may also be additional costs.

Shipping costs can take a significant bite. Boarding students increasingly rely on package delivery for their supply needs, lacking much time to shop in stores.

Parent contributions are another quiet cost. Though not explicitly required, parent contributions to the school's annual fund drive and other fund raisers are (ahem) - encouraged. Parents are also asked to provide funds for dorm "feeds" on weekends, snacks for school sports teams, and other events.

PAYMENT & FINANCING

Applicants whose families are prepared to meet the complete cost for their student's prep education are known as Full Pay students (FP). Applicants whose families require financial assistance from the school are known as Financial Aid students (FA). All else being equal, FP students have a significant admissions advantage over FA students.

Some families with an annual adjusted gross income of $350,000 and above can anticipate Full Pay. Families with an annual adjusted gross income below $200,000 can anticipate some potential for financial aid from the school, though amounts and terms vary widely, depending on the particular school's resources and the family's circumstances. Families in between $200,000 and $350,000 face even more uncertainty; some schools will help with some financial aid in this middle range, while others will not. Families with significant assets but lower income may also face financial aid uncertainty according to how each school evaluates their situations. (See Financial Aid below.)

Families must declare themselves FP or FA in the admissions application. Families that intend to be FP at the time of application but have reason to believe that they will need financial aid in subsequent years should seek financial aid at the time of application, even if they anticipate being rejected for aid in the first year.

As with colleges, prep boarding schools expect that families will make every effort to self-finance the student's education costs. The four main sources of family funding are:

LIQUID ASSETS

— Cash on hand and in family accounts.
— Liquidate holdings – selling stocks, bonds, other resources
— Reduce nonessential family expenses – car payments, gym, cable tv, clubs, classes, nightlife, shopping
— Gifts from relatives are sometimes available

DEBT

Some families with significant home equity may secure mortgages or lines of credit to cover educational costs. Others take out personal loans or educational loans to cover school costs.

Some basic advice about taking out a prep school loan – don't do it unless your family has a rock solid 100% guarantee of new funds coming in soon that will cover the loan amount. A prep school education can be a fantastic experience, but it is not essential. There are college costs coming soon enough.

SCHOLARSHIPS

Scholarships are systems of support for students based on merit. Scholarships tend to be competitive, with formal applications and often other requirements. Two leading secondary school scholarships are the Caroline D. Bradley Scholarship, a merit based program available to all students at any family income level, and the Jack Kent Cooke Scholarships, which are based on merit and family need. Corporations, nonprofit charities, and local associations are also sources for scholarships. (See Resources in the Appendix.)

Though not common, some schools offer various types of scholarships for new students; these scholarships have their own eligibility requirements (geographic origin, URMs, high academics, specific talents, etc). Many more schools provide some scholarship support for continuing students in recognition for student achievement or service while attending the school.

GRANTS

Grants are based on financial need, not merit. They are the largest source of financial aid for boarding school families. Grants come from the school's endowment and from contributions from alumni, parents, and faculty specifically dedicated to student aid.

PAYMENT SCHEDULES

One-time total payment for tuition and room and board is due ahead of the school year, typically in July. Two payment plans have a first due date in the summer for half of the cost, with the second half due in December. Monthly plans begin with a double monthly payment at the start, usually in May or June. Some schools have other schedules, such as quarterly payments.

Schools often offer a tuition insurance plan which provides coverage of tuition costs in case the student must withdraw during the school year before completing paying the full tuition. Most schools require this insurance for period payment plans.

PARENTAL FINANCIAL RESPONSIBILITY

The schools have individual policies in the case of divorce, separation, and remarriage. For example, some schools may not accept existing non-judicial divorce agreements regarding financial obligations. Parents who separate, divorce, or remarry after the student has entered the school may also face financial complexities, particularly regarding FA. Parents with such circumstances would be wise to check with each school to obtain a written explanation of specific guidelines.

SCHOOL ACCOUNTS

The schools will establish **family accounts** for tuition payments and for the billing of other costs such as medical fees, airport shuttle fees, and other one-time expenses. A monthly or quarterly statement is sent to the family.

Many schools have **student debit accounts,** similar to a bank ATM card, for books, supplies, and small purchases on campus. Some schools have arrangement with off campus stores and restaurants. The school ID card often serves as the student debit card.

FINANCIAL AID

The scope of financial aid at these schools is staggering. Consider these statistics:

-35 U.S. schools listed on boardingschoolreview.com report that 50% or more of their students receive financial aid. 183 schools give FA to at least 30% of their students.

-The Choate Rosemary Hall School reports that sixteen families with an annual income over $200,000 receive annual grants of $11,780-$40,780, with an average grant of $30,492.

-The website for Saint Paul's School (NH), reports that in 2016-2017, the school awarded $11.4 million to 216 students out of a school total of 531, including seven regional scholarships.

-Phillips Academy at Andover, MA, has 47% of its students receiving FA and 13% on "full rides" – free tuition, fees, room, board, and other school expenses.

-Phillips Exeter Academy in New Hampshire offers free education to students from families with annual incomes of $75,000 or less. According to the school site, exeter.edu, 95% of American families may be eligible for FA at Exeter under certain circumstances.

-Georgia's Tallulah Falls School, the North Central Texas Academy and Missouri's Wentworth Military Academy are among ten boarding schools with over 70% of students receiving financial aid, according to boardingschoolreview.com.

Many boarding schools have strong endowments. Others are not so fortunate and as a consequence cannot be so generous. Nevertheless, boarding schools overall have significant financial aid resources that allow families to send them their students, including many who could not afford a day school tuition.

The FA largess at some of these schools explains in part their popularity. As might be expected, competition for admissions to these high endowment schools is intense, adding another layer of uncertainty for students seeking FA as well as admissions.

Boarding school FA has much more leeway than most college FA. Under certain circumstances, families with over $350,000 net income may be eligible for notable FA.

PARENTS FINANCIAL STATEMENT (PFS)

The schools use a common FA application system called the Parents Financial Statement (PFS) which is provided by the School and Student Service (SSS) division of the NAIS. The PFS collects your family's financial data that you submit to them online. The SSS then submits that PFS to all the schools to which you are applying and from which you wish to receive financial aid. Some families adopt an admissions strategy of applying to some schools with FA and some schools without; you submit the PFS only to schools to which you are applying for FA. The PFS charges a single fee for all the schools to which you are applying for FA. This single fee also applies whether you are applying for one child or several.

The PFS is available online at sssbynais.org. After creating an account, you will be able to access a blank application and work on it at your convenience. Much of the information must be drawn from your federal tax documents.

The PFS is a detailed report of your past year's family finances. It requires an explanation of all income, with separate pages for each business or employment source plus federal tax documentation in the form of a signed, filed IRS form 1040 plus all required forms and attachments that you filed in your most recent annual federal tax filing. If you are not providing a tax return for the most recent calendar year, you must provide estimates of line items. If your student receives and accepts an offer of admission, your completed return for the most recent year must be submitted to the school by May 10. As with a tax audit, you should be prepared to provide expense and bank statement documentation should the school request them.

DETERMINING NEED

Though the family's recent tax returns are subject to scrutiny, boarding schools use an honor code system towards a family's overall reporting of income, assets, and spending. The schools expect the families to take responsibility for financing their children's education, and to make that a priority over discretionary spending. Families that seek FA but still have the wherewithal for elaborate vacations, pricey new car purchases, and lots of shopping will not get much joy from the schools. Families that spend on necessary expenses like medical and dental costs, the education of other children, the special care of family members, or costs from a family emergency or crisis will be looked on more favorably.

Income, assets, and debt obligations are looked at closely. Disposable assets bear particular scrutiny. Vacation homes and non-retirement investments might be considered by some schools as liquid assets that could be used for tuition. Others may accept the second dwelling as a nonliquid asset but refuse the second home depreciation benefit that the IRS may allow. The schools do not consider retirement accounts as part of family assets.

As with college FA, boarding school FA is largely calculated from annual family income, and that chiefly in the form of employment, i.e., compensation for services rendered. Families that own and operate businesses and derive income less from salary and more from profits, rents, royalties, or other non-employment sources, face particular challenges for prep FA, because their business inventory may be mistakenly categorized as disposable assets. Families in such atypical situations should stay in close communication with FA offices.

FAMILY CONTRIBUTION REPORT

SSS takes the data you have entered into your PFS and creates a Family Contribution Report (FCR) to give you an estimate of your Expected Financial Contribution (EFC) towards your student's education. The EFC is a total for all siblings applying to that school for that year. The student contribution is a separate figure if the student has assets apart from the parents.

The FCR is an estimate that gives you some idea of what you can expect to pay ahead of a formal notification of an FA award from any school that offers admission to your student.

The Family Contribution Report considers your income, assets, debts (including mortgage), and how many family members are in tuition-charging schools and colleges. The Report also analyses how much discretionary income you have available for school costs, after household allowances, taxes, debt service, and other necessary costs.

FCR estimates are useful but should not be relied upon as an accurate predictor. Each school's FA award decision may vary significantly from the FCR estimate because schools make their decisions based on many variables, including the school's enrollment goals, its FA budget, and the specifics of your family's financial situation.

FA TIMELINES - PLAN AHEAD!

As has been mentioned, FA timelines are not identical to admission timelines. Since FA is contingent on documentation, the family's tax documents are a critical aspect of the FA application. The deadline to file the PFS with tax returns attached is typically February 1.

Some families are so on top of their accounting that they are able to attach their latest federal tax returns with their PFS. Most, though, will file their prior year's returns. The schools will make their FA decisions based on whatever tax documentation they receive with the PFS. The schools will require the latest return by May. FA offers may be adjusted accoding to the latest figures.

THE PROS AND CONS OF BOARDING SCHOOL FINANCIAL AID

PROS

The huge resources of many boarding schools and their generous grants allow many students access to an outstanding education.

The broad reach of these grants offers a wider diversity of student backgrounds than day and public schools tend to provide.

Boarding school FA helps support families in a much wider income range than colleges do, thereby helping relieve some pressure on families looking ahead to funding college costs.

Boarding school FA typically goes to pay tuition and other direct academic costs, rather than food or lodging. In such a case, the grants may not be taxable at the federal level. Some individual states may also allow tax free tuition grants. (Disclaimer: this is not financial or legal advice – seek the counsel of your accountant and tax attorney.)

CONS

Applying for FA lowers the applicant's chance for admission at most boarding schools.

FA applications add additional uncertainty to the admissions process. The decision to award a grant, under what terms, and for how much is impossible for families to predict.

FA applications are complex, have their own deadlines apart from the application deadlines, and require information from family tax returns. These factors can add considerably more work and stress to the admissions process than may be experienced by FP families.

FINANCIAL AID FAQS

Q: Are international students eligible for FA at American boarding schools?

Most FA typically goes to domestic applicants (US citizens and legal residents), but there are exceptions according to the policies of individual schools. International students should also be aware that boarding school FA programs require verifiable income sources and often tax returns as well – aspects that are sometimes difficult for international families to provide. International students in need of FA should make sure to inquire with each school on their list regarding eligibility and resources for international applicants.

Q: Is there a difference between the Financial Aid Estimator used by boarding schools and the Net Price Calculator used by colleges?

College websites provide the Net Price Calculator so that applicants and their families can get a sense of what financial aid they might receive from that college. The NPC asks for family income and asset information to provide an estimate of potential FA.

Boarding schools use something similar called a Financial Aid Estimator (FAE). True to its name, it provides estimates, not calculations. It asks only for annual income and the size of the family. As a result, the FAE delivers a loose idea of potential boarding school FA.

Q: Do boarding schools and colleges calculate family need differently?

A: The answer depends on which colleges, but overall, yes, there are significant differences. Boarding schools always factor in other prep school tuition expenses (boarding and day) that the family is paying for other siblings. Most colleges and universities do not.

Boarding schools factor in the age of the parents who must prepare for retirement, major medical costs, and the costs of parental care (parents caring for their parents). Many colleges do not provide allowances for these family expenses. Boarding school FA excludes formal retirement plans from calculating family assets; many colleges include them. The schools' approach resembles the FA assumptions of elite colleges – the Ivies and others – which due to their resources can afford to take a more generous approach to FA calculations.

Q: Is there much deviation between FA awards from different schools for the same applicant?

There can be, especially when a family's income is atypical. Also, each school has its own variations on how to calculate FA, again similar to colleges.

Q: Do siblings receive tuition discounts at the same school?

A: Often the answer is yes. Many schools offer substantial savings to families who enroll more than one student concurrently. Check with the school to find out its policy on sibling discounts.

Q: What about COLA? We live in a very expensive area!

A: Many schools recognize that the cost of living can vary widely and make FA adjustments based on this. Some schools do not. Again, check with each school regarding their Cost of Living Allowance (COLA) policies. The Association of Boarding Schools TABS has some COLA comparisons on their site, www.boardingschools.com.

Q: What happens if our family financial circumstances change during the application process?

A: If you experience an unforeseen major change in your family finances, you need to contact the FA office of each school to which you are applying.

Q: Once we receive our financial aid package, is it set for our student's full time at the school?

A: FA is based on an annual recalculation. You will be required to fill out a PFS every year with updated family figures and the latest federal tax filing. Your financial aid package will be adjusted accordingly.

Q: What happens if we receive an offer of admission from a school but the financial aid package states an EFC that we can't afford?

A: You might contact the school for a reconsideration. This subject is discussed in detail in Chapter 9.

JUST ASK!

A typical tendency among many parents is to discount their chances of FA support. Many families with day school or college experience assume that they would be ineligible for boarding school FA and therefore do not apply for it.

In truth, boarding school FA is available to wider ranges of family incomes than is available from most day schools or colleges. Many families who apply for FA are stunned at the level of support they receive for their students.

Optimism counts – just apply and see what happens.

CHAPTER 9
DECISIONS AND DEADLINES

The completion of admission and financial aid forms marks the end of the application phase of the admission process. Phase #5, the decision phase, now begins. In its first part, the admissions officers make their admissions decisions. In the second part, the applicants and families must respond to those decisions with their own.

DECISION PHASE TIMELINE*

January 15/30	Submission Day
January to March 9	The Long Wait
March 10	Admission Day
March 10-April 9	Decision Month
April 10	Acceptance Day
May 10	Final day for FA tax form submission

*This timeline is used by many but not all boarding schools

SUBMISSION DAY ARRIVES

January 15 is a traditional application deadline for some schools; many others have deadlines on January 30 or in February. Some schools have "rolling admissions" with no set application deadline. You will need to check with each school to confirm application deadlines. FA application deadlines are usually January 31st or Febuary 1st. Check with the SSS. Keeping track of multiple deadlines is critical.

Despite calendars and careful planning, quite a few families find themselves struggling to meet deadlines. December and January is often a time of heightened, sometimes frantic, activity. The admission offices are fielding last minute calls from applicants and families. Teachers who have been slow to file their recommendations must be prodded. A missed deadline may have different outcomes depending on the school. Some schools are forgiving and will accept late applications. Others will not.

INSIDE THE ADMISSION OFFICE

Once submission deadlines arrive, the boarding school admission world shifts to a slower, studious tempo. The admission office phones quiet down, and the staffs turn to the formidable task of reviewing the mountains of applications. Though every school has its own procedures and sequences, the overall process is the same.

Each application is inspected to make sure every part is present, and the entire application is placed in an individual file. When all are ready, the files are gathered – this is the applicant pool from which the AOs must create a new incoming class and replenish upper classes. AOs who interviewed certain applicants will also review the files of those applicants.

Suitable to the winter season, the AOs now settle in for weeks of reading, analysis, and contemplation.

The AOs first identify applications that are very strong or very weak. Applications with strong hooks are set aside and fast-tracked for the final consideration stage. Applications with unavoidable deficiencies such as poor academics or low entrance test scores may be placed in a "pass" pile.

The large majority of applications are then reviewed closely, and the AOs work through each application page by page and line by line. The AOs are searching for students they can champion in upcoming group meetings, whose applications show success and the promise of more. Many admission offices have "multiple review" policies, where every application is looked through by two or more AOs.

After weeks of individual study, the AOs meet in a series of general staff meetings. The AO who first reviewed an application will present it to the group for discussion. A general vote decides whether to admit, wait-list, or deny. Sports coaches and other school insiders may campaign for certain applicants. The hooked applicants sail through first. Another portion of strong applications are easily and quickly worked through. The work slows down when decisions must be made about borderline cases.

Admission teams have set numbers of places for incoming classes. Schools with both boarding and day students have subquotas for these two cohorts. There will also be spaces to fill in each of the upper classes. Since a school's "yield" (the percentage of admitted applicants who accept a place compared to the total number of admitted applicants) is never 100%, admission offices always select more applicants than there are places to fill. This calculation is never completely accurate, as the numbers vary year to year, but each school carefully studies annual admission and yield rates. When an acceptance estimate is accurate, nearly all of the available places are taken from the "admit" pool. If a few spots remain, the AOs will then turn to the wait list. Once in a while, the reverse circumstance occurs – more accepted applicants decide to enroll than the AOs expect, resulting in a lack of space at the school.

These uncertainties affect how the AOs work with the applicant pool. If the "strong admit" pool ends up too small, the AOs will turn to the "consider" pile. If the "strong admit" pool turns out to be too large for the admission quota, the AOs must cull the pool to reduce it.

ADMISSION DAY

March 10 is the traditional date when many schools let their applicants know whether they have been accepted, wait-listed, or "not invited to attend".

Applicants offered a place have exactly one month to accept or decline. It should be noted that quite a number of schools do not use March 10 as their Admission Day, preferring to announce earlier or later according to their needs. Many have no need for a particular day at all, as they employ "rolling admissions" policies.

THE LONG WAIT

Meanwhile, back home, the wait for March 10 can seem very long indeed. Students and their families have been working on their applications for many months, sometimes years. The tremendous effort of researching schools, reviewing brochures and catalogues, attending admission events, taking the tests, gathering recommendations, writing essays, filling out applications, touring campuses and interviewing, suddenly comes to a shuddering halt on submission day and then...

Nothing. For nearly two months.

Waiting can be tedious. And nerve wracking. This is the part of the process over which you have no control. Don't make it worse than it is by obsessing over it. Get out and visit friends. Go catch up on the movies you haven't seen trying to get those applications in on time.

During this waiting period, parents need to have a talk or three with their applicant children. Remind your student that she/he has just achieved an important goal – a full application to one or more schools. Regardless of outcome, each applicant now is much more prepared to apply to college. They now know about interviewing, campus tours, essay writing, getting recommendations, and all the other details which will arise again when it comes time for college applications.

This time is also a life learning event. After all of the student's efforts trying to get into boarding school, in the final analysis, the decision is in the hands of others. As in much of life, all we can do is our best with what we can do, give ourselves credit for that, and await the outcome with patience.

You might also have another talk about another subject – the real possibility that March 10 could turn out to be a complete disappointment. Every year many hopeful applicants are brought to tears when none of their applications are accepted. Many of these schools are very difficult to get into, but every boarding school hopeful expects a good outcome despite the odds. Sadly, this is an impossibility. Disappointment is the rule, not the exception.

This can be devastating for a young person. Rejection (because that is what it feels like to the student) is very painful. It is very important that the adults in this picture – parents, family, and teachers – give the student their admiration, love, and support well ahead of the admission outcome. Once again, this process is a life lesson. A person's worth does not depend on what other people decide. Teach your student that before March 10 arrives.

Applicants coming from private day schools sometimes face a problem due to the 3/10 acceptance calendar. Many day schools have earlier re-enrollment deadlines that require deposits. This puts families in a bind. There is no blanket solution, but some day schools will give you leeway if you explain the situation in advance. Since your student needs current teacher recommendations, it is likely that the school is already aware that your student may be leaving for boarding school. Therefore it would be advisable to discuss this dilemma with the day school admissions people well in advance.

STUDENTS, WHILE YOU'RE WAITING....

Why not keep on with your applications?

I'm not kidding. If you are a data driven person you will recognize that the admit rates for many of these schools is so low that the odds for an acceptance are very shaky. The probability for making the wait list is much higher than receiving an acceptance. It makes sense therefore to plan for the wait list.

After the application deadline in January, take steps to improve your application right away. Should you get on a school's wait list in March, you will need extra ammunition to help you get off it with an acceptance. Application improvements include adding any awards or achievements – academic, athletic, or ECs, improving your grades, or perhaps taking on a new creative or charity project. Students who add to their accomplishments from Jan-March may be in a better position to get off the wait list than those who don't.

ADMISSION DAY ARRIVES

The March 10 announcement date is generally agreed upon by many schools to keep chaos to a minimum, but each school has its own way of going about announcing their decisions. This can be bewildering to students frantic to learn their fates.

Some schools announce their decisions using online portals Some email their decisions on March 10, but the times of these announcements can vary year to year. Some schools send decisions by US mail or by Fedex. Some schools announce ahead of March 10, while others announce well after March 10.

DENIALS

Admission Day will bring many letters of rejection. If they arrive amidst a few wait lists or offers, they don't hurt so much. All that is needed is one affordable acceptance from one school; if that is the case, everyone can turn their attention to considering that offer.

Of course, if all of one's applications result in denials, that situation can be painful indeed. That pain might be eased somewhat if the letters explained precisely why the school chose to deny – but they never do. Often times, boarding school rejections are the first big disappointment in an applicant's young life. Parents are advised to treat it as a learning opportunity, a lesson in dealing with outcomes we cannot control caused by someone else's decisions. If the applicant did everything possible, there is nothing to regret and the family should be proud of the student's efforts. If the applicant could have done more, lessons can be learned from that.

An application that results in all denials likely made one or both of the following errors. First, the applicant was mismatched with the schools chosen and failed to include schools with more relaxed admission requirements. Another likely cause was that the student's personality was not fully presented in the application process.

The remedy to the sting of rejection is to make new decisions and move on. One option is to keep applying with applications to schools with rolling admissions. Many great schools, including very well-known ones, accept students right on through the summer. A second option is to plan on reapplying to boarding schools the following year – either the same schools or different ones, and either for the next highest grade or as a repeat in the student's current grade. Both of these options benefit from the student's application experience, which makes for a stronger candidacy. A final option is to stay at the current school, take the lessons of this boarding school application experience, and apply them to the college admissions process.

Young people facing defeat often think that their world has ended. The sooner they pick themselves up and move on, the sooner they will learn that the world is what you make of it, not what happens to you. Admission denial may be a gift in disguise, a lesson – however painful at first – that those graced with admission success may not learn until they hit college or career disappointments.

WAIT LIST

To be wait-listed means that the applicant is deemed qualified to attend the school if/when a space opens up. A wait list offer can be a disappointment, as it is not a full "yes", but then again it is not a "no". Wait-listed applicants have a chance, but no guarantee, of receiving an offer. Most wait-listed applicants never get off the wait list. Nevertheless, even the most sought-after schools will have openings as applicants who are accepted choose to take another school's offer or decide not to attend because their financial aid is not sufficient, or because of family circumstances that unexpectedly arise. Legacy applicants usually receive a wait list rather than a rejection, as a courtesy to the family.

Wait-listed students sometimes face complex situations – perhaps a wait list from their top choice but an offer from other schools further down their list. The deadline to accept an offer of admission is April 10. Schools do not turn to their wait lists until after that. Will the school that wait-listed the student come through with an offer? Or should the applicant follow the adage "love the school that loves you"?

If you received an admit offer (or several) along with some wait lists, review your wait-list list. Are there any schools really worth waiting for? If so, ask yourself why you were wait-listed instead of accepted. The school did not reject you, but it has not shown you love either. You already have at least one admission offer. If you think that you don't want to wait, contact the wait list school immediately, tell them that you plan to enroll elsewhere, and thank them for their consideration.

If you want to stay on a wait list, be sure to contact the school(s), thank each for their consideration, express your continued desire to enroll, and assure them that you will update them with new information – higher grades, new awards, and projects. A failure to follow up indicates a lack of interest. Some schools will eliminate wait-listed applicants who fail to respond expressing continued interest.

If you have no offers, staying on a wait list has no cost. If you do have one or more offers, you will have to decide whether you want to accept an offer by April 10 with the chance that your wait-listing school may offer you a place after that deadline. In such a case, you will have to either decide to stick with the school to which you committed, or switch to the school that took you off the wait list. The latter choice will be costly – you will forfeit whatever initial deposit you made when you first accepted the original offer.

ACCEPTANCE

Acceptance is the happiest outcome, of course. Notices of acceptance arrive by email with cute "welcome" videos. Others come by mail, by private delivery, or appear online on school portals. Some are paired with calls from the Head of school, a current parent, or an alum. Sometimes students are so thrilled to get a "yes" that they want to call right away to accept. Resist this urge. Those who applied to several schools should wait to hear from all of them before making any plans. Those who applied for financial aid need to take more time to review aid offers. Even if your number one choice accepts you, and even if you have applied to that one school alone, do not commit right away. Enjoy your success, celebrate, but don't rush into this commitment. You have a full month to decide, and many unexpected factors can arise, as we shall soon see.

FA OFFERS

Applicants who seek financial aid usually receive word of their financial aid packages along with the announcement of acceptance. Wait-listed applicants seeking FA will not receive FA offers.

The school's offer of admission is not contingent upon an offer of financial aid, which is often handled by a separate department. This can result in complications. For example, a school might offer admission but with no financial aid or not enough aid in the family's view. Also, as happens, students applying to several schools may find widely ranging FA offers. What to do next is largely dependent on your particular circumstances and will be discussed later in this chapter under "FA Negotiation".

YOUR NEW LIST

You may have one offer and one or more wait lists and some denials. The denials are firm, and you should turn your attentions elsewhere. The wait lists are possibilities that won't kick into action for another month. If you have one or more offers, you should focus on these, even if you were wait-listed at your "dream school."

You may have one offer and all the rest are denials or wait lists. Even in this situation, you are not yet done with school evaluations. You need to look closely at the school that is offering you a place. Take the time to do this.

Once an applicant has received an offer of admission, the entire dynamic of the application process reverses. Before the offer, the student and family were chasing the school. Now the school is chasing the student. This can be a thrilling experience, and the school wants to make sure that everyone stays thrilled right through the deadline for committing to attend, exactly one month later on April 10.

Choosing which school to attend is a much weightier decision than choosing the schools to which to apply. The choice to attend entails major commitments – financial, emotional, academic. Who will make this final choice? The student or the parents? The person who will be experiencing the school or the person who pays for it? These questions must be answered before moving forward.

Many parents decide that the student should make the final decision as to which school to attend, reasoning that the student needs to take responsibility for this major choice. Other parents reserve the final decision for themselves. Still others try to arrive at a group decision. Whatever dynamic you think best, make that plan clear to everyone ahead of the decision process itself.

You are now focused on one decision—which school? You are no longer thinking of these schools in the abstract or in a hypothetical "what if?" posture. Now you are charged with comparing offers and opportunities. Be aware that your opinions may change radically over the course of the coming month. A school you liked but didn't love may suddenly leap to the top of the list whilst your dream school may suddenly not seem so dreamy. Even if you were accepted to only one other school, plan on going to revisit days.

REVISIT DAYS

Revisit days are an important part of the decision phase; families would do well to make every effort to attend them together. You can apply the tips cited for "Campus Tours" in Chapter 9, but you will need to change your perspective.

Back when you were thinking about which schools to put on your list, campus tours gave you a quick snapshot of the school and the surrounding community. Revisit days are much more intense and consequential. Now you have the opportunity to make direct comparisons between specific schools that have made offers of admission. Campus tours were part of your fact-finding missions. Revisit days are "fit finding" missions. The student is looking for the one school that is more suitable than any of the others. Revisits are about learning more about the culture, the feeling, and the vibe of the school, which will be the student's new home, community, and education, all rolled into one.

During revisit days, the schools make a big effort to woo admitted students and their families. So let them woo. Plan to attend revisit days, even if only one school has offered admission. Sit in on the presentations, pick up the "swag" they offer. Take the guided tours again, rethink the whole thing. Committing to a prep school is a major investment. The student needs to envision life there for one, two, three, or possibly even four or five years.

Schools typically schedule revisit days in late March and early April, with a grouping of days during one week, then another grouping during a second week. This is so because schools assume that families will be visiting several schools and will need some scheduling flexibility.

As you might anticipate, this custom has widely ranging impacts depending on which schools happen to offer admission. Some families find that the various dates of revisit days align themselves harmoniously; others struggle with conflicting schedules. If your family falls into the latter category, rest assured that the schools will make every effort to accommodate you outside of their scheduled revisit days; they have already made you an offer; they want you to enroll.

Think through your itinerary and schedule your trip(s) as soon as possible. Flights tend to be available and not too expensive at this time of year, but hotels may fill up quickly as many other families head to campus. Try to schedule your arrival for the day before and stay overnight. Families requiring financial aid may request travel assistance from the schools so that they may attend revisit days. If other circumstances still prevent the family from revisiting, be assured that many a student has gone to revisit days without the family present and many others have entered their schools sight unseen and gone on to success.

What to bring? Pack lightly, dress comfortably. Students, you are no longer seeking admission, you are in if you want to be. There's no need to dress to impress but in order to get a better feel for the school, you might dress to the school code, informal or formal. Bring good walking shoes and plan for rain. Bring this book too, plus notebooks and cameras or cell phones to take stills, videos, and audio commentary. One terrific resource: the Emma Willard School's "Best Fit Guide" on the school website:

https://www.emmawillard.org/sites/emmawillard.org/files/best_fit_guide_0.pdf

An alternative access route is to go to www.emmawillard.org, click on "Admissions", then click on "Your Best Fit – Get Tips" which takes you to the Guide.

Revisit days begin with a reception – chipper AOs will welcome you, sign you in, offer you swag, and steer you towards the breakfast munchies. Typically, there will be an official welcoming speech, after which time the students will be steered through one series of events and families will be steered through another. There will be classes to audit and tours to take. If you already took a pre-admit tour, do everything all over again: dorms, classes, sports, dining hall, everything. Sure, you will be covering the same territory, but now you will be looking at it from a completely different perspective. Earlier, you were a tourist, visiting the school to learn more about it. This time around you are considering a major commitment. Big difference.

Separating the students and families is a good strategy for all. Admitted students need to experience the school without family in tow. Also, separate classes and tours can provide more information – take notes!

Include some investigation apart from organized tours and events. Walk around the campus by yourselves. Walk around the town. Try to schedule a full day or two at each school. Rushing from one campus to another is not only stressful, it's confusing. How can you make the right choice if everything is rushed?

STUDENT REVISIT

Students, revisit days are your chance to take charge. Contact your AO in advance so that you can see what – and who – you want to see. Ask to meet enrolled students with interests similar to yours. If the performing arts are important to you, ask to tour the theatre and hopefully meet the theatre and dance instructors. Athletes will want to meet with coaches and check out the gyms and training centers. Schools will try to meet your requests, provided that you let them know well in advance of the revisit days.

Your job is to get to know the campus vibe, how the students treat one another, and how the students and faculty relate and see if you connect with all that. Best time to do another campus tour? Try for midmorning when the students are awake but still fresh. If at all possible, try to lunch privately with enrolled students, not with other admitted applicants or parents or teachers. Ask them direct questions: are you happy here? Would you apply again? What's good, what's not so good? Talk with students similar to you – gender, age, ethnicity or race; what can they share about their experiences? Talk also with students who are very dissimilar – do they relate to you, are they friendly and helpful? Remember that these encounters cannot tell you the whole or true picture of a school, but they are way better than not engaging. You may find new perspectives, positive or negative, that you had not considered.

Classroom visits may or may not be helpful; like student guides, teachers may or may not be engaging or memorable on any given day. Every school has outstanding teachers and some not so great ones, but your luck of the draw in a revisit classroom should not be viewed as critical to your final decision. Focus more on what's going on with the students. Who participates? Are most engaged in the conversation, or are only a few carrying on the discussions? Are the students huddled in subgroups all the time? Subgroups happen, it's natural, but if URMs or ORMs never engage with the general population, or vice-versa, if girls never speak to boys, you may want to devote more thought to that school's culture.

At this point, the Dean of Admission is still your Most Important Person on Campus, but now for entirely different reasons. Who else got in? Who is already there? Who will be coming up after you? The selection of the student body is the number one factor in determining your experience at the school – more than the Head of school, more than the faculty or college advisors, and much much more than the facilities.

PARENTS REVISIT

Revisits for parents can be strangely unsettling, especially if this is the second time on campus. On the first tour, parents were actively involved. Now that one or more offers are in hand, the student is now in search of the "right" school, which is a more personal decision. Parents may find themselves leaning towards a different school or schools than the student favors. Parents are advised to avoid trying to influence their students during this period – let them think all this through without parental pressure. Parents are also advised to think ahead to what should be done if there is disagreement right down to the acceptance deadline. That impasse may never come; many students and parents experience changes of opinion in the course of this decision process and come to an accord. Nevertheless, it makes sense for parents to think ahead about how to resolve the possibility of differing views.

MINORITY REVISIT DAYS

Some schools have the wisdom to schedule revisit days specifically for minority students and their families. These are scheduled a day ahead of the general revisit days and are a great way for students and parents to meet with currently enrolled minority students as well as minority faculty and administrators.

Minority revisit days often center on receptions and shows put on by the school's student clubs and teams, plus discussions about the minority experience on campus. These programs allow parents and students to get answers about their particular concerns ahead of general revisit events. These revisits are also good for the parents to connect with other parents and share experiences with the school and other schools everyone else is considering. Sometimes sharing insights about the surrounding community's attitudes can be reassuring or eye opening.

COMPARING SCHOOLS

Once revisit days are done, there is a small window of time to make the Big Decision: which school to attend next year? If you have visited multiple schools, try to get that list down to two or three finalists. Students should run the finalists through a series of direct comparisons:

Comparative fit analysis- Some schools are happier than others. How is the campus community, what are its strengths, weaknesses? Which campus felt inspiring? Which felt like a place you could call home?

Comparative asset analysis- Another selection tool is to consider each school's opportunities – academic, athletic, activities – that speak directly to your interests. If you are a dancer, how do these schools' dance facilities and programs compare against each other? If you are an advanced math student, how do these schools provide for advanced courses? Consider facilities – library, studios, labs, and sports centers – and unusual opportunities such as foreign travel, outside internships, and the like. To this add your valuation of each school's location and ease of access.

The one alternative school on everyone's list: Should be the one you are attending now. How bad is it and should you leave it for boarding school? You have likely answered this question already but ask it again – previously, you were comparing your (real) current school to a hypothetical boarding school. Now that you have an offer of admission, you are comparing two specific schools. Is it still worth the cost and effort to leave what you have at home to start at boarding school?

Students and Parents: Consider **Stepping Back** as a strategy if your choices are close but not identical in academic rigor.

Some students choose the somewhat less rigorous school to help their chances of staying in the top quartile of the class.

or

Hit Pause (stopping the process): One option is to hit the pause button. If at any point in this entire process the student feels conflicted or is not fully engaged, it might be well to put everything on hold until next year.

FA NEGOTIATION

If your top choice school's FA offer is lower than the family can accept, the family should contact the school's financial aid officer immediately to request an adjustment. The family will need to make a clear argument for this change: perhaps some unavoidable family costs did not appear on the PFS or new circumstances have arisen such as accident, illness, elder care, or job change.

In some circumstances, an applicant's preferred school has offered low or no aid and other schools have offered substantial support (in the form of a written financial aid offer). If the preferred school remains preferred, the family should contact the preferred school with this news. That school might then reconsider its offer.

Families are advised not to try to "play" the schools. Going back to seek more financial aid indicates that the family would send their student to that school if only the FA were more substantial. If a family asks a school for more financial aid and that school matches or exceeds other FA offers, it would be bad form indeed for the student to not to accept that school after all.

Applicants seeking FA usually take an admission offer from the school with the strongest FA package. If two schools have very similar FA packages, the decision returns to a straight across choice between the schools.

CHOOSING YOUR SCHOOL

If you have at least one offer, you must decide whether or not to accept. Sometimes there is a crystal clear answer. In other situations, there are multiple choices, and one is as wonderful as another. Do not agonize or worry about making a mistake. Relax and think it over. You might even return to the schools for another look or a sleepover in a dorm. Whatever path you choose, second-guessing yourself is a waste of time. "What if I had only gone the other way" is a question with no answer.

Some students know in their hearts which school is the one for them. There is no doubt. Others are torn. Sometimes, there is difference of opinion within the family. Sometimes financial aid offers must direct the decision towards a less desired school. However you get to the point of accepting an offer, make sure that the choice is one that the student agrees with. It is difficult enough for an eager, committed teenager to adjust to boarding school. A halfhearted or reluctant student may be headed for tough times.

CHOICES BEFORE THE FINAL CHOICE

There may be some decisions to make ahead of accepting an offer. One is the choice to table the boarding school quest for now; perhaps it's best to put off this quest until another year. Perhaps it's best to try out the school for one year. Perhaps it's best to stay at the present school or switch to another local one. Students, if you have doubts or second thoughts, talk it all over with your parents. Parents, listen to what your student wants. If there is family agreement, you can go forward. If there is no clear agreement, keeping talking. There may be wisdom in putting off your prep plans.

DECISION ANNOUNCEMENT

At long last, you – student and parent – make your choice of which school to attend. Once this occurs, all the schools involved – the one chosen and the ones not chosen – must be notified as soon as possible. This correspondence should be emailed, because time is of the essence. Your school of choice needs to know your decision to lock in your place; the schools you decline need to know so they can move on to their wait lists to fill your spot.

Thank all these schools. They deserve gratitude, for they chose you over many others. They also deserve respect as people and as institutions. Maintain cordial relationships with everyone at every school.
Why? For one thing, your siblings may want to apply to some of these other schools. For another, there is a possibility that you may end up transferring from your chosen school. Besides, good manners and consideration for others count a lot in the prep world. If you are new to this, you might as well start practicing now.

STAYING ON THE WAIT LIST

Wait lists have a period of high activity immediately after the April acceptance deadline. Schools go to their wait lists when accepted applicants decide to enroll in a different school. After this period during the summer, wait list activity usually falls into a lull, but as the onset of the school year approaches, there is another flurry of activity; some enrolled students get cold feet about attending or family circumstances change, opening up more spots for those still on the wait list.

Meanwhile, many students on the wait list withdraw from the list as they commit to other schools or decide to stay home. The odds of getting off the wait list are slim, but as time goes on, a student's chances increase. Some applicants get an offer from the wait list right before the start of the fall term, and in some instances, some weeks after the term begins!

If you decide to stay on a wait list, keep working to improve your candidacy. Even small improvements can help differentiate you from others on the list. If your SSAT test scores were less than fabulous, you might retake it. If your scores improve, send them in to the admissions office. The same goes for improved grades or any awards or honors. Remind the school of your continued enthusiasm.

PART IV
BOARDING SCHOOL LIFE

Boarding school affects students and families in different ways. Chapters 10 and 11 address issues for parents. Chapter 12 speaks to students.

CHAPTER 10
WHAT TO DO AHEAD OF SCHOOL

A boarding school education does not start when the new student sets foot on campus. It began way back when your family first began thinking about applying. Every step, from the first glimmer of that idea, has been part of this education. Now that the student has accepted an offer of admission, it's time to swing into full prep action.

First, **embrace this change**. The shift from home life to boarding school is a major event, the beginning of an entirely new era for your student. It is also a big change for your family. Every family member and every relationship will be affected. Getting organized for boarding school can be a fun family project and a way to transition everyone to this next life phase.

While looking ahead to your student's new school life, *carpe diem*, "seize the day." Make it a priority to spend time together as a family while you have the opportunity. Your student may want to spend as much time with friends as possible. Friends are fine, but family is more important. Take meals together, share each other's company and celebrate. In the years to come, you may look back at this brief interval between acceptance and first arrival on campus as a precious time. Use it well.

MAKE DROP OFF PLANS NOW

One important task in this phase is to decide on how you are going to handle sending your student to begin school (this is known as Drop Off) and then make the necessary travel arrangements. If your plans will involve air travel, schedule flights right away, before summer comes. As you might expect, the onset of the school year – prep and college - can impact available tickets and flights. If you wait to book tickets, you may pay quite a bit for the delay.

Before you plan your trip, you should decide – as a family – on your best Drop Off strategy. Some families travel en masse with their students to the school, help with the move in, run around to nearby stores for last minute supplies, and stay together until the last possible moment. Other families prefer the old classic boarding school Drop Off – one parent drives the student to the school, they say goodbye, and that's that (that was my experience). Another even curter Drop Off is simply for the student to ship off alone by plane or train and arrive unaccompanied. Whatever you decide to do you had best make your travel plans as soon as possible. Revisit days brought many accepted students and their families to the campus; Drop Off brings the entire student body at once!

Your travel tasks aren't done yet. You will need to decide soon about family trips to campus and your student's holiday break trip schedule. Boarding school students must leave campus during the Thanksgiving and Winter breaks. You will need to think about their travel arrangements well ahead of time. Long distance families need to pay particular attention to these two travel related issues before the fall term begins.

If your family intends to visit the campus on Parents Weekends (usually scheduled for mid October), plan on booking hotels and rental cars soon.

LET FRIENDS KNOW

If you have taken the advice to keep quiet about your boarding school quest, now is the time to let your friends know what has happened and what lies ahead. If you live in a community where attending a boarding school is not common, you will likely face a lot of questions about what they are and why you chose to apply. The school catalogue and website can answer a lot of the routine questions.

The move to a boarding school can result in changes in social relationships for both parents and students. Some friends may welcome this news; others may find it suspicious or snobbish or may even feel threatened. Eventually true friends will make their adjustments, but you can expect some formerly warm friendships may morph into cooler acquaintances.

PAPERWORK & PROCEDURES

You can anticipate a pile of paperwork to process in this period. There is no rush for most of these; many deadlines for completion are sometime in the summer months. That said, you would do well to square away everything that you can as soon as you can. If you deal with the paperwork early, you can get answers to any questions that may arise during the spring term. Boarding school staffers often are difficult to reach during the summer months.

The school will send you instructions for the student to take **placement exams** for language and mathematics ahead of the fall term. These tests will help the school place the student in the appropriate level. There is no need to prep for these tests. The student's initial level of placement can and may be adjusted to a higher or lower level once at school. Though these placement tests are nothing to worry over, the student should be fully rested ahead of the exams and prepared to give them full attention.

A full **physical exam** is required by the schools, plus proof of immunization. If the student has any ongoing medical issues, be sure to discuss these with the school well ahead of the start of the fall term. Athletes will need a **sports exam** and doctor's approval to participate in sports at school. A history of sports injuries, particularly concussions, will be required. Be aware that the student must comply with the medical rules of the school's state, not yours. Some states have quite particular regulations about athletic exams . This may result in a need for additional documentation that you do not now have available. Do not wait to complete these examinations in case regulatory complications arise. Also bear in mind that many fall sports began team practices weeks ahead of regular fall term start dates.

A student with a formal diagnosis of attention deficit disorder or a learning disability may seek **academic accommodations** such as extra time and quiet environments for exams and in-class essays. Such accommodations will require advance submission of documentary substantiation, such as a neuro-psychological evaluation. Families with students on **medications** must fully understand the school policies regarding student access to medications. Parents will be asked whether the student's refill prescriptions should be handled by the family physician or by the school doctor. The schools require that students pick up some medications daily or weekly from the health service rather than keep the medications in their dorm rooms. This is especially important as regards medications subject to abuse or unauthorized use by other students. Such circumstances are not uncommon on boarding campuses, particularly for prescriptions for ADD/ADHD. A student's breach of school rules regarding use and possession of certain medications may result in severe punishment and possibly expulsion. Parents should contact the school health service for procedural guidance.

The schools maintain **student portals** online where students can find school calendars, news updates, class schedules, and contact information for students and faculty. The student portal is set up during the spring or early summer months. Parents should make sure that their students establish an account as soon as the portal is available.

Parent portals allow parents to view their students' course schedules, weekly and monthly calendars, and upcoming events. Each of the student's courses will have a page with contact information for each teacher and class roster, plus schedules, syllabi, and other detailed information. The parent portal will list absence/tardiness information, midterm teacher assessments, end of term assessments, grades, and total volunteer hours. Parent portals open up later than student portals do, typically just before the start of the fall term. Parents are advised to study the **school calendar** to get a clear sense of the school's yearly schedule well ahead of the fall term. You can print out the school calendar from the school website.

PREPPING TO PREP

Students should use the summer to "practice for boarding school", to take more responsibility for daily life: housekeeping, laundry, time management, and a reading schedule (students have summer reading lists from the schools). Some students are already self-sufficient and organized; others are decidedly not and may resist such a plan. Stand firm – a disorganized student, however bright, will face big challenges on day one at boarding school. It makes sense to establish good life skills in advance.

Students who have experienced summer camp or extended scouting trips already have some preparation for living away from home. They are used to non-parental adult authority, taking care of themselves and their belongings, and living along with others they don't know well or at all. If your student has little experience in these activities, schedule a few mini-trips away from the family ahead of entering school.

Your student might take a trip to visit relatives or stay with trusted family friends. If such a trip involves a journey by plane or train, arrange to have your student travel alone to practice unaccompanied trips, with no friends, siblings, or cousins. The parent can see your student off and have the host adults receive her/him upon arrival. Such practice encounters can give the student some life experience ahead of boarding school and can help minimize anxiety once there. This will also give your family practice in the details of minor travel; airlines require special check in procedures for travelers under a certain age.

WORK OR PLAY?

How should your student spend time this summer? Some families let students go the vacation route, with fun trips and plenty of time to chill with their friends ahead of boarding school rigors. Others go the preparation route, arranging for tutoring to lessen the stress once school starts.

If you take the latter path, consider some summer math tutoring ahead of the first term. This will give your student a head start in math class just when he/she is sorting out school life in general. Another key area is improving reading speed and comprehension. Boarding students read much more than students at other types of schools. Some summer reading clinics – either in person or via software – can really pay off at school.

SIBLING ADJUSTMENTS

Be aware of the needs of siblings during this transition. In the tumult of prep school applications – tests, tutoring, campus visits, interviews, and the like – siblings can be sidelined and feel neglected. They may be suffering even if they do not appear to be, anticipating the loss of their brother or sister. Parents can reassure their other children that this transition is not a threat to them, nor is it a permanent loss. It helps to emphasize the upside – more parental attention for the kid(s) at home, fewer schedule conflicts, and perhaps more room in the house.

FAMILY MEETING

Sometime during the summer, schedule a family meeting. Download the school's student handbook ahead of this meeting. Everyone should read it cover to cover.

At the meeting, go through the **school's expectations** about student behavior, what constitutes major and minor infractions, and the school's judicial processes and communication procedures ahead of any issues that may arise in school. Some areas to discuss are the school's rules regarding personal conduct, permission to leave campus, tardiness and absences, and cheating and plagiarism. Your family also needs to understand the routes of communication to address various issues that may come up – what teacher or administrator to contact for problems with academics, sleep, health, or other students.

The student also needs to understand and agree to your **family's expectations**. If the parents expect a certain level of academic success, make that clear. What about personal conduct? One area where family and school rules may vary is the subject of dating and sexual activity. You will have to discuss what your family expects or allows independent of the student handbook.

In your discussion, set a **family communication policy**. The general assumption is that with cell phones, voice mail, texts, Skype, and social media, families will always be in touch with their students. This is not always so at boarding school because students are often so busy, they can't immediately respond to all messages, especially if they come from multiple family members. Equally, students need to remember to stay in touch with home. Texts work best for practical messages and questions (note – some schools ban student cell phone use during the school day). One "old school" solution is a weekly phone/Skype conversation at a set time on a set day. Some families establish a short nightly call for the first few weeks. Phone conversations are best to judge the student's mood, an aspect that's central in the first weeks of adjustment. If your student has siblings or other close relatives, don't forget to bring them into this conversation.

SHOPPING

As Drop Off day approaches, some families are compelled to channel their excitement and anxiety into vigorous bouts of shopping. As discussed in the following chapter for students, rein in this impulse. Prep dorm rooms are small, and having many furnishings can make life worse, not better, in close quarters. Prep clothing needs to be functional and weather conscious – students are outside a lot, walking from one building to another. One rule of thumb: other than uniforms or other clothing required by the school, whatever the parents buy for the student ahead of Drop Off Day will go unused. This subject is discussed in the following chapter for students.

Put **name tags** on all boarding school clothes. This step will be critical if you plan to use a laundry service – clothing without name tags is much easier to lose. Boarding students often borrow each others' clothes, and who owns what can be quickly forgotten – tags help. Name tags are easily purchased online. The iron-on no-sew type are very easy but tend to fall off after repeated washings. The classic sew-in type is best, but you must be willing to do the sewing or get someone to do it. Why not recruit your student to help sew in the tags? Some parents swear by indelible markers, but you need to test some to find good ones. Some markers bleed in the wash, and some fade quickly.

SERVICES

Set up **basic services** in advance. Amazon Prime is a service many students use for package delivery, movie downloads, school books, etc. Uber and Lyft accounts can be very useful on weekends. The family may want to set up a separate student **bank account** with a debit card; many schools have in-school debit card accounts so students can pay for on campus items – snacks, books, etc – without carrying cash.

At many schools the **student ID card** doubles as a debit card for on campus purchases and at some nearby shops and cafes off campus.

Many schools offer you a choice of signing up for an outside **laundry service.** The alternative is for the student to handle laundry chores with coin operated machines on campus. Laundry services tend to be expensive, and you must plan ahead to get your laundry ready to be picked up. If you miss the pick-up, you are out of luck until the next pick-up.

Laundry services offer a basic service – usually clothes are washed and folded but not ironed – and also offer additional services for additional fees: ironing, mending, dry cleaning, etc. Items usually come back on time and ready for use; sometimes items get misplaced. Having name tags on everything helps reduce the risk of loss.

Doing your own laundry avoids these mix-ups, saves money, and promotes self sufficiency. The major cost of the do-it-yourself method is time. Because of this, you might try the laundry service for the first term to focus on your course work.

THROW A PARTY

Here's a suggestion: just before your student heads off to boarding school, throw a party. Have your student invite friends, and invite the parents as well, to celebrate this new adventure about to begin.

WRITE A LETTER

Here is another suggestion for parents: before Drop Off day, sit down and write your student a letter. No, not an email or a text. A real old fashioned letter, by hand, not typed and written in ink, preferably on fine stationary with a proper envelope. In this letter, express your love, your admiration for your student, your excitement about the future, and your assurance that you will always be available to talk and help. If you plan to drop off your student in person, give this letter to your student when you leave. If your student is travelling alone, pack it away in the luggage or send it by mail. It will be read many times over in the days ahead. Very likely it will be kept long after school and may well outlive you. It will mean more than you will ever know.

CHAPTER 11
BOARDING SCHOOL PARENTING

As Drop Off day nears, parents will begin to feel the downside of boarding school. The reality of what's about to happen starts to become clear. Your student will be off entering a new phase; you and the rest of your family will face changes as well. If you have other children, they will become more of the focus in the family. Spouses often find there is more time to spend on themselves and one another. There is often a sense of conclusion that the family life has ended in some way. It has not ended, it is changing.

Parents need to prepare for a change in parent/student dynamics, at least as far as this boarding school adventure is concerned. Once your student moves onto campus and the school year begins, you will no longer be responsible for either daily oversight or rule setting and discipline. Those duties will be the school's responsibility. The parent-student dynamic, with parents holding all decision-making power, shifts to an educator-student dynamic, wherein the student's decisions are central to their prep experience. This will come as a shock to some parents and also to some students used to having parents in charge. Boarding school students must learn self-reliance, tolerance, and cooperation in ways that they may not yet have experienced at private day or public schools or at home.

This division of adult functions can be very helpful to teen students; they continue to receive love and support from their parents, but abide by the daily regulations set by the school. Many parents report relief that they no longer have to be the law enforcement figures. Many parents report a stronger, closer relationship with their students, who often come to better appreciate their parents once away from the family.

Most central of all, parents need to prepare to let go. It can be very difficult to get a phone call from one's child who is homesick or has suffered a painful disappointment. There is a feeling of helplessness when your student ends up on crutches from a sports injury or in the infirmary with the flu. Parents are hardwired to help and protect their children, but boarding school parents learn to keep these instincts in check.

The loss of control is paired with a sadness similar to what parents of college bound students feel. The student's room is still there, but the student has moved on. There is a sense of time hurtling by, not only for the student – who was only in kindergarten five minutes ago, it may seem – but also for the parent, who may feel very uncomfortable thinking through the life changes ahead. This time of troubles does not last forever. Parents usually adjust after a few difficult months. Some can't do this and become "helicopter parents", forever hovering, endlessly calling school officials, asking for more attention, intervention, changes of grades, changes of dorm room. Others, whether they hover or not, act to resolve the absence of their child and go so far as to rent or even buy a home near the school

DROP OFF DAY

Families have but one chief purpose on Drop Off day, and that is to help the student get set up in the dorm. You will likely get help with moving luggage from the dorm students or the school maintenance staff. There will be time to duck out to a store for some school and room supplies, assuming there are stores nearby. You might help out arranging the room, but rein in any urge to take over.

If your student's room is a double, the roommate will also be moving in. As a general rule, whichever roommate arrives first gets the first choice of bed. Make it a point to meet the roommate and especially the roommate's parent(s) if one or two are present. This is partly to get an idea of who the roommate is and learn something about the family. It is also partly to determine which family will be carrying the load for the other.

This merits a brief explanation. At boarding schools, roommates are paired purposefully. International students are matched with domestic students, so that both will learn from each other. Long distance domestic students may be matched with students from nearby the school. In every pairing, one family will be more advantaged geographically than the other. Usually, the nearer family will visit more often and will be in a position to be the substitute parent on behalf of the other – to invite the far family's student along on outings and report back to the other family about how their student is doing. At move in, the parents can determine which family will be doing more hosting on behalf of the other.

Help your student get set up, but don't linger in the dorm room. Give your student your letter (if you follow the advice from the previous chapter), say your goodbyes, and leave the campus. You will have to do this anyway. The schools ask families to depart campus by late afternoon, ahead of school meetings. Before this, your student needs to bond a bit with the roommate and meet the dorm leaders and other dorm residents. If you hang around, you will be in the way.

Yes, parents, this may be painful but don't let it show. Parents who have trouble parting with their children can become embarrassments to their students, who are striving mightily to appear cool and calm. The focus must be on making the student feel comfortable. Best to just give a kiss and a good hug, say goodbye, and go. Once you are away from the school, you can cry your eyes out if you have to.

If the brief ballet of arrival, room setup, and goodbye is too abrupt for you, add some extra time on the front end by booking a hotel a day or two earlier. That way, everyone can stroll the campus together ahead of check in day, nerves can settle, and there will be some time for some meals and sightseeing in the area. Just keep the final goodbye at the end short and sweet.

On the subject of local sightseeing, it's a very good idea to get to know the community surrounding the school; it will be a sort of home away from home over the next few years. You will take some comfort knowing the area where your student will be living.

Finding interesting restaurants and stores will bring you added pleasure, and you may make new friends in the local community.

You can also take solace from your communication options – phone, text, and Skype, too. Also, there will be time to visit very soon; Parents Weekend is in mid October. Families are also welcome at weekend sporting events. One word about visits – stay away for at least a month. Let your student go through the initial transition process on his/her own.

SUPPORT TEAM COMMUNICATIONS

Now that your student is squared away in the dorm, your next task is to develop connections with the network of campus professionals who are now responsible for your student, acting as surrogate parents in your stead. You will want assurances that your student is in good hands, that the staffers are competent and reachable by phone, text, and email.

You can attempt to do this ahead of Drop Off day, but faculty and staff are difficult to reach at that time. Drop Off day itself is too chaotic to manage much more than a brief introduction to the dorm supervisors, and it's unlikely they will be able to remember you or your student in the flood of new arrivals.

The best plan is to begin your connection campaign after the adults have had a chance to meet your student and put a face to the name on the dorm roster. Understanding which staffer does what will help you know to whom you should go with various questions or requests. Texting seems to work best, rather than email.

Dorm supervisors, or house masters, are your main contact for any residential issues.

Academic advisors are problem solvers and can help your student with such typical first month issues as establishing homework routines, time management, and personal organization. For any larger issues, the advisor can route you to the proper **student support specialist.** These specialists are available for an array of issues – time management tutoring, nutrition and eating habits, emotional and psychological counseling, and physical therapy, among others. The campus health service can answer questions regarding your student's prescribed medication or anything regarding illness or injury.

Coaches are another source of contact and feedback. If your student came in to school as an athlete, you may be in contact already. If not, it's fine to contact coaches directly rather than through the advisor. Your student's dorm or house will also have **parent volunteers** who assist the supervisors with dorm activities.

There may be times when you need to contact dorm supervisors and advisors immediately. Make sure you enter their cell phone numbers into your phone's contact file. Do not hesitate to text or email them when the occasion requires it. This is not intrusive - these professionals are used to urgent parental messages. The faculty tends to be less available on demand and slower to respond. For your questions or comments on larger school topics, it's best to direct all of your questions and concerns to either the dorm supervisor or the advisors and let them pass on your comments to the appropriate office. For major issues, contact the Dean of Student Life. As you proceed through the first term, you will develop a rapport with the school's adult supervisors. You will likely hear more from them than from your busy student!

MANAGING YOUR OWN TRANSITION

Now comes the hardest part for boarding school families. Life goes on, but that bedroom is empty. The house is quieter. You feel the loss of your student. You hope this ache will go away, that life will return to the way it was. This is, of course, impossible. A major shift has happened and there is no going back. There is only going forward.

Your first step forward is to know, or at least hope, that you will be able to adjust to this new phase, that the pain of loss does soften over time, and that you have given your student a wonderful life opportunity. You will always miss your student, but you have my assurance that the intense pain you may experience at first will abate.

Meantime, be resolved to present an enthusiastic disposition towards your student's experience. No matter how hard it is for you, you must be positive when you speak by phone. If you don't think you can do that at first, communicate by texting. Once again, you must take a backseat to the student's transition. Starting at prep school is never easy, and the last thing a student needs is to be distracted worrying about a grieving parent back home. Offer praise, encouragement, and patient advice; keep a tight rein on your own issues.

SOME REMEDIES

The most effective way to handle this situation is to find positive, inspiring activities to inspire you. A child away at school means more time and energy can be spent on other children, your spouse or partner, and even (heavens!) your own life. How about a vacation on your own – even it's a four hour "staycation", going out to dinner and a movie?

Now may be a time to begin some new creative endeavor, to reach out to friends you have not seen in a while, to volunteer for charity work, join new social groups, or attend concerts and art shows. A decision to get happy is no disrespect to your student; it's actually a direct help. Boarding school students take comfort from knowing that all is good on the home front, and likely will enjoy hearing about your new activities and projects.

Some parents find that a new pet can help this transition; other parents turn their attention to their other children; still others focus on preparing "care packages" of baked goodies and other treats. Some parents establish contact with other prep parents through social media or online chat rooms such as collegeconfidential.com's Prep Parents subgroup (inside the Prep Admissions section) or by joining school sanctioned parent organizations.

PARENT ORGANIZATION

Family involvement with boarding schools used to be plain and simple. Parents dropped their students off at school in the fall and picked them up in the spring. Parents were also invited to show up for sporting events and performances. Academic assessments were sent by mail. Really big issues – illness, accident, or misbehavior – might involve a phone call. That was it.

Nowadays, the schools have extensive parent organizations to provide support for the students throughout the academic year. Parent organizations provide volunteers to host admissions receptions at the school and in cities around the world; assist with revisit days and other school wide presentations; provide each dorm or house with one or more parent volunteer to provide drinks and snacks for school sports teams, and serve the school in myriad other ways.

By necessity the parents organizations are primarily composed of parents of day students. They are an excellent resource for long distance parents seeking information about the local area – lodging, restaurants, historic sites and other places to visit. The organizations maintain lists of local parents affiliated with each dorm or house as well as lists of local parents by region, so that parents living near one another can connect. Parents are encouraged to help support "feeds" on Saturday in the dorms and to sign up to provide funding for sports teams' drinks/snacks. The parents' groups also host parent events on campus at various times during the school year.

VISITS & BREAKS

The schools schedule periodic weekends for family visits. These events are not required for parents, but they are good opportunities to visit with your student and connect with the school community. **Parents Weekend** takes place in October. The schools put out rather elaborate programs, usually including lectures and exhibits, an array of classes in various subjects taught by school faculty, school sports, and performing arts presentations. Parents sign up for teacher conferences to meet their students' instructors, who give a brief overview of the student's progress in the course. The weekend is rounded out with social events.

New parents may sign up with the expectation of extended time with their students. Often, though, students have major homework and sports commitments and only a little time for their families. What parents do get is a closer connection with the school community and opportunities to chat with the dorm supervisors and advisors as well as faculty, coaches, and administrators. If the student is playing on a fall team, parents also get a chance to see their student in a sporting event. If they do not already know, parents and families get a firsthand look at how hectic a highly scheduled prep life can be.

Parents are also invited to a **winter event** at many schools, especially the parents of 11th grade students who are beginning their college admissions quest. As with Parents Weekend in the fall, there are performances, sports events, and opportunities to meet with faculty and staff.

At most schools, students are required to leave the campus during the major breaks – **Thanksgiving, Winter break and Spring break**, which tend to be longer than breaks at public and day schools. Most students travel home for these vacations. The schools tend not to assign homework during the breaks; they are true vacations. Athletes needing continued training and those students with extended individual projects may need to continue their daily regimens.

Parents often report real changes when their students return home. There's more maturity and assurance in evidence. Especially for the first home visit, keep your vacation plans loose. Returning boarding students usually have one major objective – sleep. Let them sleep.

STORM PREDICTIONS

Boarding schools can be trebly stressful for the students, combining the intensity of the campus experience and a steep maturation curve with the ordinary throes of adolescence. One of the very first things that the schools do at the opening of the fall term is to inform the new students about counseling services. Professionals are readily available to help with most issues – academics, emotional and psychological issues, diet, and time management. Student prefects and listeners are on call as well. New students who are unused to this level of support may not reach out when they need to. Parents should keep in phone contact with their students at the start of their boarding school experience. Your chats may be short and unimportant – this does not matter.

What you are doing is establishing a phone routine which can act as a safety valve when problems arise. Sooner or later they will call about:

Panic: Entering the boarding world can be disorienting. This is normal and temporary. Tell your student to relax, have patience and take things one day at a time. Steer your student to one of the student prefects. For further assurance, text a heads up to the dorm supervisor to consult with the prefect.

Homesickness: At some point, your student may begin to regret this move to boarding school. The old life back home looks better in the rear view mirror. You can help your student by your assurance that school will get better and that home life will be there on breaks and vacations. Your regular phone chats and other communications will help ease the heartache. Care packages work wonders.

Many students feel intense isolation once at school. Suddenly they are without family, without friends, without context. The process of meeting new friends can be slow, but give them assurance – they will meet other students who will become friends. Again, patience and perseverance are key.

Exhaustion: Boarding school takes a lot of energy. Those who are disorganized, who don't sleep well, or who are stressed often suffer from sleep deprivation. Some of this can be resolved with time management, and some of it with sleep counseling. Students who are exhausted can not think properly. Exhaustion requires intervention from counselors who can help students get the sleep they need.

Failure: In the public and day school world, failure is to be avoided at all costs. In the boarding school world, failure is central to education.

Boarding school can be very challenging; it is full of outstanding students who excel in different ways but everyone fails at something. Reassure your student that failure to achieve something worthwhile is not a fault, that there is honor in the attempt and from failure and disappointment, we all can learn resilience, determination, and persistence. Encourage him/her to shake off the disappointment, and if the opportunity arises again, to try again. As a boarding parent, it is difficult to receive such phone calls, to hear the suffering in your child's voice. It's best to remember that adolescence is always stormy whether or not the student attends a boarding school. Your voice on the phone will give great comfort.

Depression: Some students suffer debilitating melancholy by the end of their first fall term or early in their winter term. This may or may not be related to their school situation. Ongoing depression is not something to minimize or to ignore. It is a serious condition that requires immediate professional attention. Tell your student to contact the advisor and the health service right away. Follow up with those advisors yourself.

Do not hesitate to contact the adult advisors to discuss your student's issues. The staff has the experience and they are on site. From afar you cannot accurately gauge the scope of what may be going on. Often what seems a matter of grave import disappears quickly; other problems merit continued attention or intervention. Self-control and emotional resilience are difficult lessons that many students don't fully face until they go off to college. That's part of what "prep" means at boarding school.

OTHER MATTERS

RELIGION

As discussed, historically most American boarding schools had a religious (Christian) aspect with daily chapel and full Sunday services. Today religion is an option on most campuses, with only a minority still affiliated to a faith. The towering chapels that still dominate many campuses are now used by many faiths, including ones never seen in the classic prep era, with religious leaders as adjunct staff to lead services and advise students.

Some campuses are more conducive to religion than others, with lively well attended services and warm faith-based social groups. If yours is a religious family with regular attendance at weekly services, you may need to discuss your expectations with your student. The super packed school schedules and the lack of time and sleep may require students to be much more determined to attend religious services on campus than at home. Additionally, because of the multiple faith schedules, many students find that their religious service is held at odd hours. These factors, combined with the fact that other students will avoid services of faith by choice, may dampen the resolve of students of faith. A compact with your family promising at least weekly attendance at a service is one way to help promote if not entirely ensure your student's continued religious practice.

WEIGHT GAIN

Your student may experience the prep equivalent of "freshman fifteen", a sudden weight gain in the first term away at school. In the old days, boarding school food was a scarce commodity, served three times daily but without additional access to snacks during the day.

Some students of old took to raiding the kitchens in search of ice cream, aided often by kindhearted kitchen staffers who "forgot" to secure the kitchen and freezer doors. Nowadays a boarding school campus is a snacker's paradise. Everywhere you look there are cookies and other treats, most of them empty carbohydrates that need no refrigeration and provide a sudden brief sugar rush, ideal for body water retention and extra pounds. Many students ease their initial anxieties by snacking, hoarding stashes of comfort food in their rooms. Even if the campus is devoid of munchies, local pizza moguls hover nearby awaiting the call to deliver.

Parents need not fret overly about this. Sudden weight gain typically goes away as the student relaxes into the campus routine. Boarding school requires a lot of physical effort – walking from classroom to library to classroom, climbing the stairs in the dorms, walking to town, and required sports daily. Even a small adjustment of food intake can result in a big burn off of calories. If weight issues persist, students can turn to the school's nutritionists and psychologists.

FIRST TERM CRASH AND TUTORING

It is not unusual for incoming students to experience a marked drop in grades during the first term. This is particularly so for students entering after the first prep grade level. If this happens to your student, you likely won't know about it until midterm teacher assessments are released. Sometimes new students don't have a clear idea of how they are doing in their classes, or they don't want to know, or if they do know, they don't take steps to get help.

If this happens, keep calm and resist any urge to micromanage. Such a circumstance is a normal boarding school opportunity for student maturation. There will be time to adjust by term end and time after that to improve the overall yearly grade. New students are provided with many academic support systems: advising, teacher consultations and peer tutoring. Your student should take advantage of all of these, time allowing. Check with the advisor to monitor your student's progress.

If these methods fail, you might then bring in additional weaponry – outside tutoring. Subject tutoring is narrowly focused. The tutor identifies the student's specific weaknesses in the course and helps address these. Test tutoring preps the student for upcoming general tests – PSAT, SAT, or ACT. Schools often allow tutors to come onto campus to tutor their students in a common area such as the library. One-on-one tutoring can be very effective, but it is expensive. A lower priced alternative is online tutoring. Online companies offer packages of hours which can be used for several subjects and by several members of the same family. The student is assigned a tutor and schedules live consultation by Skype and online interface in one, one and a half, or two hour increments.

OFF CAMPUS PERMISSIONS

Typically, students are allowed to walk or bike to business areas immediately adjacent or very near to campus, if such exist. More extended travel, by bus, cab or Uber, to more distant towns or to visit the homes of day students, will likely require specific parental approvals.

In the initial stage of your student's boarding school experience, general parental approval - allowing your student to travel without your explicit per-trip permission - is not advisable. Your student has more than enough to handle just adjusting to campus activities. Off campus jaunts are distractions and have the potential to lead to questionable results.

Concurrent with keeping a close rein on off campus permissions, do not give blanket permission for your student to ride in a private vehicle. If a circumstance arises wherein a day student parent may drive your student somewhere, it is far better all around that you must be contacted directly for specific permission, to avoid any misunderstandings. Permission for your student to be driven by another student should never be granted.

COLLEGE APPLICATIONS

One major aspect of boarding school life is the college application process. The schools have experienced professionals to advise and guide the students. Parents are largely ancillary to this process despite their role as financial guarantors.

Usually, counselors will meet with the student, in group sessions and individually, to craft a college admissions strategy, based on the student's transcript, SAT or ACT test scores, and extracurricular resume. Many schools use the Naviance system, which compares the student's data with the schools' recent matriculation data to determine probabilities of admission to various universities. The counselor and the student will then work out a slate of prospective universities and colleges.

Parents have little to do with this process, other than perhaps to accompany their students to college visits, and many students handle even this task on their own. Parents are advised to regard this marginalization as a sign of maturity, as the student takes more control of their own future.

However, parents need to bring their students back to reality about the costs involved. Lacking family financial information, college counselors can focus only on admission success not necessarily on affordability. Parents and students need to get serious about college costs. As discussed in Chapter 8, college financial aid is not as generous as boarding school aid. What kind of college expense can the family afford? Should the student aim for high cost/high prestige schools requiring heavy debt, or honors programs at lower range schools with strong merit aid?

Parents need to talk about these issues with their students ahead of college admissions plans devised by the schools.

PARENT CONTRIBUTIONS

Schools usually ask parents to contribute to annual **parent contribution campaigns**. Parents who are paying full tuition may take exception to these requests; so too may parents of limited means whose students are on financial aid. All should take note that no boarding school tuition completely pays the full cost for a student's education. Even full tuition students are subsidized by an additional 30% to cover total student costs. Of course students on financial aid are subsidized at higher rates. Plus, "total student costs" are merely operating expenses and do not include the physical school itself, its buildings and grounds and infrastructure, all of which were provided by the generosity of those who came before.

This places an ethical obligation on parents to contribute in accordance with their means to help the schools maintain the quality education they provide. This is not only a question of hard numbers, though total contributions are very important. What this does speak to is community involvement – where every parent, regardless of financial means, makes an effort to support the common good. Even small amounts have impact, as the percentage of participation counts significantly regardless of the amounts given.

Parents can become deeply connected to their students' schools. Some parents volunteer for various school projects, serve as tutors and admissions volunteers, or end up teaching or working as school staffers. Several schools have parents on their boards of trustees or serving as legal or financial advisors. Long after their students have gone on to college and careers, many parents maintain close connections with school communities.

Boarding school parents pay a great price for their students' educations, both financially and emotionally. The payoff is the lifelong gift of a superb education. Parents may find that there is another long term benefit from their sacrifice – an ongoing connection with the school community. Other children may want to attend the school; so may other family members. Deep prep family roots may grow diagonally – nieces and nephews go on to attend, then the line slants back to grandchildren. The parents may not have the satisfaction of youthful school memories, but what they may gain is a sense of fulfillment about the future.

CHAPTER 12
EXTRA CREDIT!! ADVICE FOR STUDENTS

Okay, students, this chapter is about your issues, not your parents. You are the ones headed for boarding school and you could use some advance notice of what's up ahead. But what information do you need, and how do you get it?

It would be wonderful if this book – or any book – could answer all the questions that incoming students have. That is just not possible. For one thing, very specific questions won't help students in very different circumstances. For another, specific school conditions can change quickly – an answer that is helpful one year may be obsolete the next. One book that has value despite these drawbacks is the *Boarding School Survival Guide* (2014) which offers brief commentaries on a range of prep subjects, each from a single student's perspective, from the years 2013-2014. The book is no longer accurate in some instances, but a new edition could fix that. Other sources are blogs and online communities. Some of these are lively discussion groups, but it's difficult for newcomers to sort out the good advice from the truly bad. Online advice is easy to access and it's free; but a lot of it is worth just that – nothing.

So what to do? Best advice: go directly to the source – the returning students in your new school, those who are a year or two ahead of where you are now. They are the ones who have just dealt with your particular circumstances, and have the information you need. So talk to them!

Ask the boarding school for a list of your classmates with contact info. Identify some students from your city or region. Most will be willing to help new schoolmates. Get the inside scoop from them. Maybe you can meet. If not, email or talk on the phone. If you have trouble making contact, call the school for help.

For now, you are concerned with the time before Drop Off day and what happens right after that.

GET PREPPED TO PREP

You're going to boarding school soon – but not yet. You still have classes to attend this spring at your current school, exams to study for, and sports and activity commitments. Even if your friends are coasting along waiting for summer break, strive to excel. Anticipate that come fall, you will be with new friends who seek excellence at every turn.

Enjoy your hometown friendships, but know that once you leave for school, some of these may tend to fade away. When you return on holiday breaks, you can get together again, but sometimes there will be less closeness than you had before. Some of your friends may not understand why you are leaving, or what great opportunities you have waiting ahead. They may feel hurt, or even upset, as if you were rejecting them personally. Keeping up with them on social media will help, and a call now and then can keep your connection alive.

After the spring term is when you should shift into major prep mode. Think of your summer home life as practice boarding school. First, sit down and read the school's **student handbook,** which usually is available in pdf on the school website. You need to understand the rules of the school. If you break any of them, ignorance will be no defense. Also, your school will send you your **summer reading list**. Get the books and start reading right away. Do not put this off. Boarding schools require much more reading and writing than public schools or day schools. It's better to get used to this now. Read every day, and aim to increase your reading speed and comprehension. Buying a speed reading software program might be a good investment. 7 Speed Reading, www.7SpeedReading.com is a highly rated, low cost program worth checking out.

Over the summer, your school will contact you to sign up for the **student portal**. This will be your main organizing site while at school. The student portal will contain a school calendar, your list of classes for the fall, contact information for your assigned teachers, advisors, and dorm supervisors. Later on, you will be able to look at your grades, absences, tardies, and teacher evaluations on the student portal. Your parents will have their own portal, which they can use to check your schedule, your grades, etc. Many schools also provide a list of students in your grade with photos and contact information. The student portal is an important tool for every boarding school student.

You will receive a list of **required text books** and their ISBN (International Standard Book Number) designations. The ISBN is a unique book coding system; each book, and every new edition of each book, is given its own ISBN. This is important because you will need the exact edition of the assigned textbook. Use the ISBN to make sure you buy the edition that has been assigned, rather than an older edition from a previous year. Text books are usually available on campus at the school store – but at top prices. If possible, get the syllabus for each of your classes as far in advance as you can, and see if you can buy the texts online at a discount and then have them shipped ahead of your arrival. Check with the school to ask if used texts are acceptable to save even more money. For better deals on new and used textbooks, try online sites such as amazon.com and chegg.com. Some sites will also offer textbooks for rent.

If you don't know already, learn how to do your **laundry** before you start at your new school (you may be planning to pay for a laundry service at school, but even if you do, there will be times when you will need to do laundry yourself). This involves a bit more than simply turning on the machines. Learn how to separate clothes by colors, and what wash cycle to use for which clothes: delicates, wash and wear, normal, or heavy duty. Also, it's important to know how to fold your clothes properly. Get this right, and you will avoid a lot of wrinkles and not have to do as much ironing, oh, right- learn how to iron, too. Also, learn basic sewing so you can sew a button back on or make minor repairs.

Room upkeep is a big issue at boarding schools. You may already have good housekeeping habits, but if you presently live in chaos, try to practice keeping things neater. At some schools, you may face regular room inspections; at others, maybe not. Either way, getting used to having your room in order will go a long way to helping you stay focused and efficient (and probably help a lot with getting along with your new roommate).

If you have not yet done so, set a **time schedule** for yourself and stick to it. Buy an alarm clock and use it – set your wake-up alarm at night and then actually get up when it goes off in the morning. NOTE: Do not rely on your cell phone.

Put **name tags** on all your clothes. This step will be critical if you plan to use a laundry service – your stuff will get lost without tags. Even if you plan to do your own laundry, tags are still advised. In the dorms students often borrow each others' clothes, and who owns what can be quickly forgotten – tags help with that. Use your new sewing skills to sew in the tags. Indelible markers are used by some, but these can vary quite a bit in how well they work.

Like the colleges, boarding schools maintain **scholarship and fellowship programs** for deserving students. New students should be aware of their schools' opportunities before arrival; this information can be found in the student manual or on the school website. If you think you will want to apply, use the summer to plan a proposed project for funding. Scholarship and fellowship applications tend to have deadlines in the fall, and many new students fail to apply because they are too focused on immediate move-in issues.

Many of these programs are competitive, with application deadlines. Scholarships, which are financial awards based on academic excellence or other stated criteria may be awarded by the administration based on faculty recommendations of students demonstrating outstanding academic performance. Others require students to apply for consideration. Fellowships, which provide funding for specific scholarly activities, always require applications. School travel opportunities – such as work/study in far-off countries – are also competitive and have application deadlines.

If you have been assigned to a shared dorm room, contact your soon-to-be-roommate if you can. Besides a general introduction and phone chat, talk about your hopes and plans for school and something about your living habits. You don't need to establish all your room rules right now, but it helps to start a conversation about such topics as room tidiness, quiet times, study habits, and other topics that will affect both of you.

WHAT TO BRING?

General rule: Keep stuff to a minimum, and keep it modest. Don't define yourself by what you wear or own. You will be judged by what you do, what you value, and what you aspire to.

Clothing needs depend on school dress codes. "Formal schools" have prescribed dress codes, which actually make campus life a lot simpler.

Download the clothing list from the school website. For "Informal schools" you will need everyday school clothes – shirts with collars, chinos, and sweaters for boys; slacks, blouses, and sweaters for girls. Photos on the school website will guide you.

Both informal and formal schools have one or more dressy events each term; also, you may be invited to spend a weekend with a new friend's family – and they might actually dress for dinner. Boys should bring one good suit, and girls should bring a couple of dresses and a few pairs of heels.

Basic rule: bring enough everyday clothes for nine or ten days, enough so you will have clothes to wear while waiting for your other clothes to return from the laundry. Don't bring your entire wardrobe. Pack as if you were staying for a few weeks. Dorm rooms are often cramped, as are their closets. Once you get to school, you will see what you really need, then have it shipped from home or order stuff online. Winter clothes can wait – bring them from home at Thanksgiving break, or have them shipped when the weather turns.

Another basic rule: boarding school clothing is about getting across campus to class in all sorts of weather. This lifestyle is not about fashion, it's about practicality. You will need rain gear, a parka, and shoes or boots for rain and snow (depending where your school is). Layers are the way to go – taking a layer off or adding on as you shift from frigid winter or torrential rains to stuffy classrooms.

What about furniture? Boarding schools usually will send you a list of room furnishings that the school will provide: a bed, desk, a chair, a closet. Maybe you'll get a lamp and a reading chair. The rest is up to you. You may dream of decorating your room with all kinds of cool things, but take care to stay within the school rules (student handbook, remember). Some schools allow rugs over their bare floors; some schools have wall-to-wall carpeting and you won't need extra rugs.

General advice on room furnishings: don't bring any. Dorm rooms are often cramped – you will need to see the space in person to figure out what other stuff you could or should add to it. Is there storage space under the bed? Do you need more hooks or hangers? Rugs, bookcases, a reading chair, lamps, hangers, and storage boxes can be found at stores near campus or online after you move in. Many schools have restrictions on wall hangings or ban them altogether due to fire safety concerns. Unless you are on a team, don't bring sports equipment. A basic truth: most of the stuff you bring you will never use.

Avoid extra electronics – for starters, you may not have much space for them in your room. For another, you probably won't have time for recreational tech devices. And many schools ban televisions, video games, etc. as unwanted distractions. Also bear in mind that many schools ban small electric devices in dorm rooms, like heaters, hot plates, refrigerators, coffeemakers, etc. Check with the school ahead of time.

WHAT YOU REALLY NEED

First up is stuff you might not be thinking about: **travel gear**. If your school is several hours away from your family home, you will be spending many hours a year in transit. For your luggage, avoid hard shell suitcases; there will be no space for them in your room. Go with duffel bags or softsided luggage that you can stow compactly. One possible exception is an old fashioned footlocker which triples as a coffee table, extra seat and a storage unit, For plane and train trips buy a sleep mask, good ear plugs and a neck roll, that crescent shaped beanbag thingy that helps you sleep in a sitting position.

These items are also very useful on the school team bus, especially coming back from an "away" game at a distant school. They also come in handy in your dorm room if you want to sleep when your roommate is still up with the lights on and making noise.

Tee shirts and underwear – Boarding school kids go from class to sports to clubs to study hall. You may end up getting dressed, sweaty, showered, re-dressed, muddy, soaked, showered, and dressed again – all in one day! Have plenty of tee shirts and underwear at the ready.

Fan(s) – Boarding schools now have fantastic facilities, but central AC is still a rarity. Dorm rooms are notoriously hot, even in the most northern climes. The best defense is to have some fans. The rectangular window-mounted fan is a favorite to suck out the hot dorm air. A tiny desk fan can be a welcome adjunct, to get a breeze going inside the room. Fans (window fans especially) quickly sell out in nearby stores. Order these in advance and bring them or have them shipped ahead of your arrival.

Also critical to buy in advance: **bedding**. Your bed will likely be a single XL (extra long), so get a good pillow or two, a nice comforter, 2-3 fitted XL single sheets, and a XL single mattress pad. Boarding school beds are hard; that pad will be a blessing. Don't wait to buy this stuff at a store nearby the school – the pads and sheets will sell out fast. If there are colleges in the area, these items sell out even faster. Check with the school to confirm the dorm mattress size.

Useful small items to bring with you or buy near the school: a fix-it kit – needles, thread, small screwdrivers, scissors, needle-nose pliers , some packing tape or gaffer's tape, string, and a bit of wire; some bolster-type pillows to turn your bed into a couch; a robe and flip-flops for your trips to the shower; extension cords (the round kind from BB&B); and that small alarm clock separate from your cell phone.

Computer stuff – some schools provide what you need. Deerfield gives each student a Mac Air laptop and lends out iPads in certain classes. At most schools, you will be expected to bring your own computer. (FA students often receive funds to buy a computer.) Check with your new schools' IT department about their specs. You may need to upload certain software. Make sure your equipment is ready to go on day one – you really don't want to have your laptop in the repair shop once classes begin. Get the school's advice about having a personal printer. All schools make printers available to students, either in the library, in the dorms, or other places. Do you need one in your room, and is this allowed?

DAY ONE: WHAT TO EXPECT

Boarding school can feel bewildering and disorienting at first. You are going to feel a range of emotions: happy, sad, fearful, lost, and excited. This is healthy – all this is new and your feelings are going to respond to all of the changes. Also, at least you are not alone! Other new students are feeling the same things, and though the returning students may look relaxed and confident, they faced the same issues when they were new.

Best general advice: be patient, everything good takes time. Proceed step by step. Progress comes in small packages. Since time can seem endless to a young person, try breaking it down into smaller pieces. Just get through Day One. Then go for Week One. Then Month One. Each has its own challenges. Day One is a very practical day, with lots to do.

CHECKING IN

Whether you come with your whole family, or just take a bus from the airport by yourself, you will begin your boarding school career by checking in with the school, usually at a major campus building. If you don't know where your room will be ahead of time, you will be given a dorm assignment, as well as probably a packet of information and maybe some school spirit "swag". Most likely, a student guide will lead you or point you to where you need to go.This is an exciting time, with scores of new students, many with their families, all eager and anxious to begin their lives on campus. Many boarding school alumni recall this special day fondly and in great detail.

MOVING IN

The first challenge you will face is moving in. Prep dorms typically have several stories and lots of stairs. Elevators are pretty scarce on most campuses. Some schools make sure that upperclassmen or school staff are available to help new students move in.

Usually schools have "move-in hours" during which family members, friends, and dorm supervisors are around to help, carry, unpack, and run errands. There is a cut off time when non-students have to leave campus. Goodbyes are said, and then your boarding school career really begins. This will likely start with a dorm or house meeting where all the residents – students and faculty – will meet to get acquainted and to discuss dorm rules and procedures.

ROOMMATES

For students assigned to shared dorm rooms, the next challenge is the roommate. In past decades, most students had some experience with communal living before boarding school, either at home with siblings, group cabins at summer camp, or tents on scouting expeditions. As these traditions have faded and private homes have become larger, fewer and fewer new boarding students have had any room sharing experience. For many new boarders, sharing a bedroom will be a "first".

For a new boarding student, roommate assignment is a random relationship. You may click, you may not, but you will learn how to get along with others you don't know or maybe don't even like. Living with someone else can be a challenge that requires tolerance, patience, and negotiation.

On Day One of rooming together, or Day Two at the latest, you and your roommate should have a meeting to establish room rules. First, make some decisions about private space and boundaries. It's wise to keep all the personal surfaces private. For example, keep your desk, bed, and dresser for your stuff only. Talk about noise and light, especially after lights out. Some kids may think they have the right to Skype away at any hour of the night because their relatives live six time zones away. Be explicit. You can't expect your roommate to know what you want or need. If you need quiet at night to concentrate on studies, say so. If you tend to be messy, say so. Try to talk through all basic room sharing issues – sleep and study hours, visitors, using phones and Skype, room tidiness, and who has which bed and which closet. Be as accommodating as possible but don't allow yourself to be pushed around either.

Roommates can be great fun at first; someone who could be your BFF. Don't count on it, though. Your initial impression may change. Living as you now are in a sort of teenage fishbowl, sharing one's secrets or problems with just anyone at school is ill-advised. Keep your own counsel. Your roommate is not your confidante, and in the months or years to come, may not be your friend at all.

Equally, learn to keep confidences. If your roommate tells you something very personal and private, keep it to yourself. If you pass on private information, you can expect that it will get passed on again – and again and again – until your roommate hears about it and knows that you betrayed her/his confidence. That in turn will get around, and your reputation will suffer.

Keeping secrets is a big deal at boarding school. Protective silence is considered a central tenet of group loyalty. Preps guard one another, especially with regard to adult authority, and expect everyone to comply with this law. To go against it is a Capital Prep Crime (and the dramatic issue in many a movie set at a boarding school). That said, there are specific situations that require a student to resist this code of silence and alert authorities of a bad situation. Such circumstances are discussed below under "Misbehavior".

HOUSEKEEPING AND LAUNDRY

If you have followed the advice from earlier in this chapter, you already are accustomed to orderly dorm room living. If you have ignored that advice or followed it only haphazardly, you are now faced with the task of getting organized immediately. No small task.

The simplest way to manage your stuff is not to have much stuff. Boys usually get away with the most minimal of wardrobes; girls perhaps not so little. Whatever you do, figure out how to store your clothes with some kind of system – hangers, shelves, boxes, drawers – that will simplify your life. Boarding school students are completely scheduled from dawn right into the night. There is little time to spend cleaning up your room, so you need to keep it neat all the time.

Laundry is another prep preoccupation. New students who have chosen laundry service must learn the schedule for pickup and delivery, calculate their clothing needs in the meantime, and make it a habit to double-check the laundry when it returns. Usually, these services are efficient and worth their price in convenience, but individual items do get lost sometimes; you will need to alert the company if you are missing something. Once in a while, you may also end up with someone else's hoodie or socks (which should of course be returned, not appropriated).

Do-it-yourselfers need to locate the washing machines and dryers. These may be in another dorm. Laundry supply dispensers and change making machines may or may not be available. Do-it-yourselfers need to find time in their schedules for laundry chores, usually on weekends. Fortunately, laundry chores and homework – especially reading time – work well together.

TAKE THE ROOM MESS TEST

Many boarding school dorm rooms are disaster zones. These tend to be inhabited by kids who struggle academically. As a quick experiment, ID some top students and visit their rooms. You will likely find order and calm. Is this correlation (just a coincidence) or causation (cause and effect)? An orderly environment is linked to orderly thinking and study habits. Take a few photos of these organized rooms with your phone. If you can, replicate this order. If you can't, at least strive for it. Boarding school is tough enough without fighting through chaos.

WEEK ONE: WHAT TO EXPECT

Okay! You made it through Day One. If your family came along to your move-in, they have left by now. This is your real first experience as a boarding school student. You are still in busy mode, and your to-do list will be pretty long. Here are some tips to remember:

MEET THE ADULTS

Make a point of meeting and getting to know your dorm supervisor/ house master and your advisor. These adult leaders are central to your residential experience. It may take a while to feel relaxed and comfortable with them but start these relationships right away. You will need their experience, advice, and help throughout your dorm life.

BE SOCIAL

Make it a priority to meet other dorm kids, especially the leaders. They will be your go-to resource for all sorts of issues. Offer to help with any dorm projects. This isn't sucking up, this is getting connected and putting your focus on action and progress. When you are giving to others, you don't have time to worry about yourself.

GET ORGANIZED

Your room should be in order by now. Next, do the same with your time management and your academics. Boarding school logistics have an added dimension: location. If you figure you can get some homework done in between class B and class C, you will need to figure out where you will be and what space you can use in the time you have. Many schools are so spread out that these logistics are not easily solved. Again, ask the dorm leaders for tips.

Some schools have time management advisors to help students get organized. If yours has such staffers, contact them. The more efficient you are, the better your grades will be and the more time you will have for fun stuff.

GOOD DORM MANNERS GO A LONG WAY

Your behavior in the dorm will play a major role in how you are viewed by other students and adult supervisors. Pay special attention to your manners and social awareness.

Rule number one (actually numbers 1-5) – pick up after yourself. In your room, keep your stuff organized, and even more importantly, keep it strictly on your side of the room if you have a roommate. If you do your own laundry, clean up after yourself – remember to take your laundry supplies when you leave, don't "borrow" other students' supplies, be sure to clean out the lint traps, and don't leave your wash or dryer loads sitting in the machines. If you have several loads to do, don't hog all the machines – leave some machines free for others. In the restrooms, keep the sinks clean and remember to take your toiletries with you when you leave. In the common areas, always pick up your belongings and throw away your trash.

Rules 6-10 – Help out around the dorm. Pick up after others. If you see trash lying around, throw it away. Grab a broom to sweep a porch. Cooperation and good citizenship get high marks at boarding school. You will be viewed favorably by your supervisors (which is good) and by your dorm mates (which is very good).

LEARNING ACCOMMODATIONS

If you are a student with ADHD/ADD or learning differences, check in with your advisor about accommodations as soon as possible after you arrive at school. Your family should have made arrangements ahead of your fall term, but do not expect that everything will go smoothly at first. Some of your teachers may not have been informed about your situation. Provisions for extended testing, which often results in allowing you to test outside of class periods, may not yet have been established. Students on medication for ADHD/ADD need to have their physician prescriptions registered with the school health service. As each school has its own policy regarding prescription drugs, students on medication must carefully abide by these rules. The misuse and abuse of ADHD stimulant medications is a serious problem on prep campuses and you will be held accountable if your medications are misused. Some schools allow students to keep prescription drugs in their dorms rooms. Others require the student to come in to the health center every day to receive that day's dosage.

COMMENTARY: WHO ARE YOU? (again)

Upon arrival at school, a new student can feel very alone and apart from family, in a strange world amongst strange people. What happens next is the discovery of quite a different sense of self. You may be apart from your family but you represent them. Your school may have felt strange but now when you go to town or other campuses or when you travel, you represent the school as well. Your schoolmates and your teachers are your main tribe. Within that, you are also a member of subtribes. You are not alone, you are more connected than you ever were before. And what you choose to do can affect a lot of other people.

STAY IN TOUCH

Call your family weekly, at the least. Do not wait for them to call you. Text your friends, do not call them or take their calls. It's tempting to chat away, but friends can really suck up your time. Texting allows you to control the time and circumstance of the exchange.

MONTH ONE: WHAT TO EXPECT

During the first month, you will be setting your regular routines: academic, athletic, dorm, and social life.

DEVELOP HEALTHY PATTERNS:

New students suddenly have far more freedom than they had at home. No parent hovers to dictate what to eat, or when to sleep or study.

Many newbies quickly get into trouble with this newfound freedom. Their health declines, they become sleep-deprived, and their grades tank. Instead, decide to take charge of your life. Watch what you eat – cut down on sugar, carbs, and general junk food. Get enough protein, fruits and vegetables. Make sure to stay hydrated.

Sleep is a big issue for teens. Late night texting and videos will trash your body quickly. You will be more successful if you go to bed early. This may appear counterintuitive, but think through this advice: if you go to bed early, you can wake up more rested than if you go to bed late. You will be able to get up with time to have breakfast; both the rest and the nutrition will make you more alert in your first class. There are other benefits. Going to bed early avoids two perils of dorm life. First, more time is wasted late at night than early in the morning. Getting up early allows for quiet study with less of the interruptions that often occur in the dorms late in the evening. Second, early bedtimes avoid late night snacking which is a prime cause of unneeded weight gain. Keeping an early schedule requires more studying and homework during pockets of time during the day, but the benefits are significant.

KNOW YOUR SUPPORT SYSTEMS

Often, new students are not used to relying on teachers and staffers for help outside of class and outside of the dorm.
The whole notion of seeking help from adults can seem completely alien. If this is your stance, get over it.

Boarding schools schedule regular student/teacher consultations. Go to them. All of them. If you have any difficulties in a course, talk about them with your teacher. Most likely, dealing with course problems will take up all your scheduled consulting time. But even if that's not how it is, even if everything is going great, go in to talk over what else you can do to excel. It's available, your parents are paying for it, do it.

Learn about your school's additional support systems: tutoring, emotional health counseling, medical services, nutrition, time management, sports training, music instruction, general advice. Boarding school education is available in and out of the classroom, and what you can get outside of class can be life changing.

EXPAND YOUR SOCIAL NETWORK

By the end of your first month, you will have established connections inside your dorms. You will have met your teachers and your classmates. These contacts are circumstantial. Some of these early friendships will start to fade in the first month. Seek friends beyond people who happen to be close by. Keep widening your circle of acquaintances. Find successful, established students to emulate. What are their study patterns and social networks? If possible, start up some study groups with sharp, hardworking students from your classes. You aren't looking for best buds in these groups, you are seeking a high level of academic commitment to challenge and stimulate you. If you have not yet done so, join some school clubs and sports teams.

ROLL WITH IT

Boarding school can be a great experience, but let's get real – it's still high school, and high school has jerks. You are bound to come up against negative encounters – rude behavior, bigotry, cruel remarks. Plus, you will surely have some low emotional points – insecurity, fear, and homesickness. These feelings are not easy to deal with, but they will pass. Try to keep on and not let the negative get the best of you. Coping with and overcoming adversity is a fundamental aspect of adulthood. At boarding school, you start to learn some of those lessons. This is not to say that you should put up with abuse or extreme bad manners. If something comes up that you feel is troubling, speak with your dorm advisor. If you are not sure if you want to or should do this, consult a student prefect/proctor.

Strive to be pleasant and tolerant. Boarding schools bring all sorts of different personalities together coming from all sorts of cultures. Be friendly, but not too friendly until you find true friends, ones that are loyal and trustworthy. Keep being open to meeting new people.

BASIC ACADEMIC ADVICE

Boarding school is high school in some ways but not "high school" in others. Sure, it spans high school grade levels and bridges you from junior high school to college. What is different are several critical underlying assumptions.

First, the common "slacker" pose found in many a public and private day high school doesn't cut it at boarding school. No one cares about your James Dean impersonation. Be prepared to work your tail off or you will soon be gone. Second, the high school stance that adults are the enemy is another canard. Boarding school instructors aren't punching the clock and doing as little as possible; nor are they watching the clock and just waiting for retirement. Most of them are exceptional educators. Get to know your instructors and ask for their help and guidance. So this is high school, but not. You will be better off thinking of it as "practice college". Shake off your old habits and adopt a college mentality. Part of this has to do with understanding the work. Print out your course syllabi and study them. Be clear what reading material you must complete and by when. Know the dates of tests and due dates for projects. Get into the habit of "reading ahead" of the in-class lectures. You should be far enough along on your reading that the class lectures serve as review sessions. By reading ahead, you will have had time to think about the material before it comes up in discussion, which will enhance your comments in class, another plus.

Cramming for tests is a recipe for mediocrity at boarding school. The work is too demanding and your time too limited to ace courses with last minute study binging. Instead, find small chunks of time. You will better absorb what you read if you read continually, if only a page or two at a time. You will be learning throughout the day as your brain processes the material even when you sleep. Try alternating study styles: introvert style (studying alone) focuses on visual learning; extrovert style (find or create a study group) uses auditory learning – conversation/discussion.

Boarding schools have guidelines for essay writing: how to read a prompt, how to construct a thesis statement, and paragraph structure. If this does not come easily, get writing tutoring or guidance right away. If you let this go, you may suffer lower essay grades due to format and structure issues you could have fixed from the get-go. Expect to edit your essays several times. This means you can't put off essays until the night before the due date. Schedule an outline, then a first draft a few days later, then a rewrite a few days after that, with a final polish/edit and proofing set for when most students just get started on their first and only draft.

Get very organized. Use day planners and calendars. Use alarm clocks and egg timers - schedule tasks by the hour, half hour, and quarter hour. Find your school's time management consultants and get them to boost your efficiency. The earlier you adopt these habits, the stronger your academic future will be.

TERM ONE: WHAT TO EXPECT

As the weeks and months pass, you will be settling into your school, finding your friends, and figuring out your place in the community. During Term One, stay close to campus. Stick with your studies, your sports, and your clubs. Runs to stores and town are fine, but pass on trips to big cities. Better for you to get really settled before getting distracted. A lot of new student families tend to visit on Parents Weekend and other fall events – football games and the like. When your folks come, welcome them and take care of them. This is their school too (they are paying for it, after all). Show them around, make them comfortable.

As the winter break nears, be prepared for the Big Crash – a wave of sadness, loneliness, homesickness, or a sense of loss. This does not happen to everyone, but it happens to many. Part of this may be a response to your new, still strange life at boarding school, part may be because of the season as the days get shorter and colder, and part may be just teenage angst. Some students hit this phase before the break, some just after at the start of Term Two. If it hits you, try to be kind to yourself, and seek out friends to talk to as well as adult counselors. This anxiety is a part of growing up. It's painful, but it passes, and, you are not alone. Others will understand your struggles as they struggle also. You can help each other when these moods hit. Loyalty and community are the prep way. If you really get depressed seek help from the school health center.

PREP VALUES / UNWRITTEN RULES:

Students do best who accept the unwritten rules of boarding school culture:

Stiff Competition, Fair Play, Grit, Loyalty, Service, and Team Identity. If you make an effort to meet people, help out in the dorm, and find ways to contribute to the school culture, you will be noticed (sooner than you think) and rewarded.

One downside: prep grit can go too far. If something is really wrong, it is better to talk it out – whether with friends or adult supervisors. How to decide if your issue is really serious? Talk confidentially with a student proctor, who is usually an upperclassman trained in such matters.

DURING YEAR ONE

How you, the individual student, navigate the intricacies of your particular school is a subject too specific for this book, but there are general aspects that you likely will encounter in your first year and which merit commentary.

ACTIVITIES

Extracurricular activities (ECs) are at the heart of boarding school culture, providing recreation, community service, religious and political affiliations, and social events. They are an important way to create and maintain friendships, and they provide informal mentoring and learning experiences. Some advice might be helpful:

SIGN UP for several clubs. Clubs are the best way to meet new friends, as everyone is there by personal choice, not by random selection or course scheduling. Don't worry about signing up for too many clubs at first. You can always drop out of some later on. Just go, check out different groups. You never know what might suddenly grab your interest.

THREE KINDS OF CLUBS should be on your list. School **service** clubs include school publications, campus tour guides, and student leadership groups such as prefects and student counselors (sometimes known as "listeners"). The **culture** clubs include any performing arts group, pep and spirit clubs, and any group that entertains or enlivens the campus. **Personal interest** clubs range anywhere from debate to culinary to camping to robotics to investments and beyond.

School service clubs are usually the "power" clubs, where student leadership is centered. Traditionally, those in school publication leadership – the editors – are afforded campus wide respect and privileges. Service clubs get students on the administration's radar, and club leadership goes a long way towards enhancing a college application. The culture clubs lack some of this gravitas, but they are often wildly popular among the appreciative student body and a great way to meet people and become known on campus. Personal clubs can be rewarding as hobbies and serve – like the service and culture clubs – as explorations into possible careers.

After the first month, students should have whittled down their club affiliation to three or four clubs. Though some new students might think it best to postpone club involvement until after getting settled, in most cases it is better to get involved sooner than later. Boarding school hierarchies tend to be quite corporate, and club officer positions tend to go to those who have joined early and then patiently volunteered year after year. Seniority counts. Even sports team captainships tend to go to the steady, persistent loyalist, not the super talented newcomer.

JOINING VS. CREATING

Established ECs, such as the school newspaper, are studies in politics. A student wishing to gain an editorial position must navigate around others also seeking these favored few positions. How to demonstrate one's skills and talents, gain the approval of higher-ups, and work your way up the "corporate ladder" is a mini-education in itself.

Sometimes, due to personality conflicts or a packed field of candidates, opportunities in some clubs may be limited. Instead, a student might elect to join another club or, in some instances, create a new one. Club creation can be more work, but there are benefits – you can hire yourself as club president and initiate projects. New club formation requires school approval, and a faculty member must agree to serve as club advisor.

OUTSIDE ACTIVITIES

As you rise towards twelfth grade, you may want to strike out on your own and create projects off campus. Film productions, stage shows, book projects, and art exhibits can showcase student work out in the larger world beyond the campus. Given the typical packed schedule of boarding schools, these outside projects must be scheduled carefully, usually during school holidays or during the summer months.

Similarly, off campus service commitments must fit into school realities. Local service work in soup kitchens or at Head Start and the like may be manageable as part of a student's school week – often on weekend days – but anything nonlocal would again require scheduling during holiday breaks.

As a rule, schools want to have some oversight of student projects off campus. Overambitious plans that would likely be too complex, too risky, or too large in scope may meet with school disapproval. Students are advised to pitch their project to their schools well in advance of the proposed project dates in order to gain the school's assent (and quite possibly financial support as well).

SOCIAL LIFE

Social life in all its aspects is central to the boarding school experience. Being fun and friendly is a survival mechanism. Boarding school students live their lives in close association with one another – as roommates, classmates, and teammates – with 24 hour adult supervision. Education, nutrition, and relaxation are collective experiences. At every turn, students are prompted to pitch in, join in, help, serve the community. Petty feuds, so common at day schools, are disastrous on boarding school campuses.

Conflict in general is anathema – word gets out, the adult supervisors are alerted, and the students caught up in what was a private dispute suddenly may find themselves in a community spotlight around the clock. Students quickly learn to de-escalate disputes, and to resolve them privately and discreetly. Geniality is a learned trait which will serve you well in the adult world of work.

PSST, YOU'RE BEING WATCHED

At boarding school, you are under a lot of scrutiny, maybe more than you might think. In the hallways, on the campus, in the dining halls and in the dorms, teachers and advisors are keeping tabs. So are doctors and nurses, tutors, coaches, administrators, and student prefects. Room inspections, lights out infractions, trips to the health center, problems with sleeping, eating, homework, roommates, and misbehavior – someone is going to notice.

This has an upside. Your service and leadership will be noted and sooner or later rewarded. So will character – courage, kindness, integrity. There's nothing magical about how schools choose some students for recognition. You are being observed within the prep community and judged by your actions. Behave accordingly!

POWER STRUCTURES & ELITES

Boarding school students are an elite group, but there are elites within elites. Initially, students with ongoing friendships – who grew up or went to school together – have their "bros" to hang with. Legacy students, especially those with sisters or brothers already at the school, often exude confidence and a sense of "ownership" of the school. Eventually, these "power kids" are superseded by students who excel in academics, activities, and athletics (note that some sports are particularly favored). Students in leadership positions are favored by the administration whether they are popular or not.

In general, family wealth does not play as central a role at school as it does in general society. Away from the usual status markers – mansions, private jets, luxury cars, certain zip codes – students from privileged backgrounds tend to blend in on campus. Their rooms are as cramped as the next student's, their clothes are similar, and they have as little time as the next kid. In fact, much of the appeal of boarding school to well-off families is this relative anonymity. At boarding school, everyone must sink or swim on his or her own merits. It's also a chance, a rare one, for high wealth students to meet and get to know peers from other economic strata.

This is boarding school, however, so word gets around campus. It can be a bit disconcerting to discover that the boy across the Harkness table from you is from the family that donated the building you are sitting in. It can be downright unsettling to hear that so and so's family has sent one of their private jets to whisk her off for a two day ski jaunt in Aspen, or on to the private family isle in the Bahamas. If you are a new student from modest means, these disparities of family resources cause you significant anxiety at first. Fortunately, boarding schools maintain Old Money standards about wealth, which means not talking about that subject. At many schools, a large cohort of students receive financial aid, and at some, a majority do. Who is on FA and who is not is not a subject for casual discussion, and in many cases is a cause for peer censure if someone does raise it.

FRIENDSHIPS

If you have been looking forward to making new friends at school, be patient. Finding friends can take time. Note also that your school friendships may be campus centered and may not extend into your regular life or your friends' lives. As noted these schools include students from a wide range of backgrounds, and while preps learn to bond with one another, it does not necessarily follow that their families will. Many families are not interested in inviting "new" people into their circle, except perhaps as occasional guests. (This tension may explain why *Brideshead Revisited* and *The Great Gatsby* are perennial prep favorites.)

ROMANCE AND DATING

Romance certainly blooms at boarding schools, but is less common than one might expect. The fishbowl nature of campus life has a lot to do with this. With privacy rare and gossip rampant, opportunities for romantic episodes are infrequent and most students are too busy, too tired, or too careful to get involved with someone they have to see several times every day. Schools vary widely in their rules and attitudes towards dating and sexual contact. Some take a very strict stance, with rules such as no persons of the opposite sex in dorm rooms (visits known as "parietals"). Other schools have very few restrictions. These rules are made clear in the student manuals.

Some boarding school romances endure and wedding photos turn up in the class notes in the alumni magazine. Usually though, campus romances do not last and some create real complications. Love is a powerful emotion, which can create major distractions in prep lives. Plus, dating is very time consuming, like adding another class – relationships take time, effort, and commitment. The lack of time is often cited as a prime reason for the "hook up culture" of many boarding schools, as some students seek quick emotionless sex in lieu of romance. This behavior can have serious consequences. Sex is a powerful force that can affect your emotions, your health, and your reputation. The best advice is to keep a romance sweet but not intimate. Your school community operates as a substitute family with the faculty and staff as substitute parents (in loco parentis). You will meet these same classmates over and over on campus until you graduate, and afterwards you will meet them at alumni events. If you still insist on an active romantic life, it is best to date off campus, in your home town, or at another school. That way, breakups have less consequences and your private life is less likely to become the grist for school wide gossip.

CLASSMATE TRAVEL AND VISITS

One aspect of social life on campus happens off campus when students invite schoolmates on trips or take them home for weekends. These invitations may be somewhat complex socially, as the host student must make arrangements with his/her family, the guest student must get permission from his/her family, the guest family will likely contact the host family, and the school must sign off to release both students for the weekend.

Students who are invited need to be mindful of all of this, make sure all the parents are in agreement, and plan on displaying exquisite manners during the trip. Bringing a small gift for the hostess and a follow-up thank-you note, handwritten on good stationary, are advisable. There is something somewhat starchy about prep visits; this is due to the wide-ranging composition of present day student bodies and the uncertainty of "fit" between the guest student and the host family. In older days, boarding schools were populated with students of very similar backgrounds and many of their families were previously acquainted. Now, there is a certain potential anxiety in such visits. Being genial, courteous, tidy, and helpful goes a long way to reassure everyone.

FOOD

In the long ago past, boarding school food had the deserved reputation of being awful. Jokes about "mystery meat" did not swerve far from reality. These days, campus food has improved considerably, though not completely. Nutritionists and professional chefs have upped the ante, and a wide diversity of students bring requests for cuisines from around the world.

Though some schools still maintain sit-down meals and table service, most schools use cafeteria style systems, with a range of food options to choose from. This gives students more choices, but there can be consequences. Many schools require "personal health" courses which include healthy eating habits.

Calls for improved food have brought some improvements such as the use of organic and natural foods, more vegetarian and vegan options, but those hoping for really outstanding food service may be disappointed. At basis, boarding schools view food as fuel, essential to keep the whole campus engine running. Those seeking aethestics should consider starting a cooking club or find solace in restaurants off campus. If you have true dietary requirements that are not being satisfied, do speak up; schools usually will find a way to provide the foods you need.

SERVICE

Community service is required at boarding schools. A minimum amount of service hours must be logged during an academic year, and many students will undertake longer, more ambitious projects during summer break. Service is intended as a contribution for the greater good, as students serve and learn from others less fortunate than themselves.

As with many well laid plans, service can go awry. More than a few students have figured out how to use a few days helping to feed undernourished children in an exotic land to disguise the real point of their trip, a cool vacation. Even those who genuinely pitch in to do serious charity work may be motivated by their college application resume, not a desire to help others. Such ploys rarely work. College AOs have seen just about everything and can quickly sniff out who is sincere and who is not.

Service need not involve long trips to foreign climes. There are needy communities close at hand, often quite nearby the schools. These local opportunities count as much as foreign service, and their proximity means your work can be done more often and to more effect. If your school is not working in local communities, there may be opportunities for you to create a club to remedy this absence.

Service works best with specific, achievable goals, with the cooperation of all involved, and with a fundraising structure for future work. This bears similarities to a start-up enterprise, with a business model, a budget, a timeline, clients, and measurable results. Instead of thinking of service as a nuisance or a chore, reframe it as a business opportunity. There will be a significant return on your investment – honor and merit in the doing of it, a sense of satisfaction, and benefit to many people in need. Community service may also turn into a lifelong habit, if you do not already have it. Some students even move on from their volunteer experiences to careers of service.

AFTER YEAR ONE: WHAT TO EXPECT

By the end of the spring term, you probably will feel more comfortable at school. During the summer break, you may feel less comfortable at home. School begins to feel like home; home feels like being away. You will be a veteran now – incoming students may call you up seeking help!

Fall term in your second year, assuming you attend for a second year, is often much better than the first year. Returning to campus may be very comfortable, and seeing your school friends may feel like a welcome reunion. If this is pretty much how it works out for you, you are in the right school and your future on campus will be bright. On the other hand, if the prospect of returning to school feels grim and downbeat, you might consider transferring out. Boarding school life should rewarding and even fun sometimes. If you don't want to be there after a full year of residence, there may not be a good fit between you and the school.

As you rise to the upper grades/forms, your course requirements will loosen and the opportunities for choosing more **elective courses** will increase. Remember all those fantastic courses listed in the course catalogue you read as an applicant? You probably will be able to try some in 11th grade or possibly 10th. Electives give you the chance to try out a subject or a specialty that you might want to consider as a major when you get to college or one that you might never get a chance to take again in a million years. Serendipity is a powerful force in the universe; sometimes taking off far from the beaten track can lead you to brave new worlds as yet unheard of and unknown. Steve Jobs' famous comment about his calligraphy class at Reed College is the epitome of this argument – he credited that course with assisting in the creation of the original Macintosh computer. Think through your **extracurricular activities** as well. They could end up being much more important in your adult life than you might think. In my boarding school days, I wrote for the school newspaper, worked on plays for the theatre club, and shot a film as an independent project. I ended up doing all of those things professionally.

Similarly, consider how you spend your **summers and vacations**. Should you fixate on college admission or explore career paths? Should you set your time aside for sleep and relaxation, or go all in for intense research or a creative project? Should you schedule long treks to foreign climes? Devote volunteer hours to a worthy charity? Attend sports clinics? Whatever you do with your free time, do not fritter it away. Use your time well.

COLLEGE

Boarding schools provide superior college counseling. Many college counselors (CCs) bring experience from working on the college admission side and maintain ongoing relationships with college AOs. This clubby atmosphere benefits students as the pros share information back and forth – what certain colleges are looking for at certain times and which students bear close attention from the colleges. You will be given individual attention; each student is assigned a CC, who helps craft a college list based on the student's academic record, test scores, and sports and activities successes together with his or her long-range college and career objectives.

In truth, these advantages are sometimes matched at elite day schools. The critical advantage lies with the "soft skills" at which boarding school students excel. Some of these are found in the classroom: effective communication and discussion skills, critical thinking, and independent thought. Some are more germane to boarding experience: organization, self reflection, decision making, confidence, and self advocacy.

For all the benefits, applying to college from boarding school has some liabilities – there's always a flip side, isn't there? The level of peer competence – let's not call it competition – is formidable. The colleges are well acquainted with the diversity of the student bodies within these schools, but no college is going to accept a huge number of students from one boarding school - those days are long gone. The irony of this situation is that boarding schools strive mightily to aggregate this elite cohort of students who then get in each other's way en route to college admission.

BOARDING SCHOOLS AND COLLEGE PRESTIGE

As you likely know, the current college admission world is caught up in a general mania as students desperately seek entry to certain colleges that are considered prestigious. If you feel yourself getting anxious about your college prospects, think back on your boarding school admissions quest. Were you applying to schools based on prestige alone? Did that prestige matter to your success and happiness once you arrived on campus? To whom did your school's prestige matter? How much use is your school's prestige in your college quest?

The hard cold truth is that boarding school prestige may matter only to a few people scattered around the prep world. How about the college AOs themselves? Will your attendance at Boarding School Z gain you automatic admission to the college of your choice? Obviously not. If you can accept that, apply the same general concept to the colleges. Will merely graduating from Stanford allow you to gain any job you want? Will attending Yale make you eternally happy?

Despite what you may have been told for your entire life, you are not on the road to college, you are on the road to the rest of your life. College – and by "college" we are talking here about undergraduate college – is a mere way station along your path. If Princeton has a fantastic program that you want to explore, apply to Princeton. If Colgate, Pitzer, and SMU also have great programs in your field of interest, apply to them as well. If you learn anything at boarding school, learn how to be yourself, and from that how to gain the confidence to go after what you want. Regardless of what values others hold, apply to those colleges that could help you along your journey. If one option doesn't open up, another will.

The morbid obsession with status colleges is the subject of a raft of books, that might inform your college admission efforts:

Frank Bruni. *Where You Go Is Not Who You Will Be.* New York: Grand Central Publishing 2015. Bruni's bestseller refutes the widely held notion that admission to elite colleges is critical to career success.

William Deresiewicz. *Excellent Sheep.* New York: Free Press/Simon & Schuster 2014. Deresiewicz eviscerates meritocratic admissions, describing how superior students are trained to focus on complying with the demands of college admissions and career politics, ignoring more basic questions of personal growth and values.

Ross Douthat. *Privilege*. New York: Hyperion 2005. NY *Times* columnist Ross Douthat explores the cross currents of student life on an elite campus in this memoir of his undergraduate years at Harvard.

Daniel Golden. *The Price of Admission*. New York: Crown Publishers 2006. Golden's best seller, based on his Pulitzer Prize winning reports in the Wall Street Journal, lays bare the ways that college admissions pass by qualified candidates in the admissions process of elite colleges.

Harry R. Lewis. *Excellence without a Soul. (2006)*. Philadelphia: Public Affairs/Perseus 2006. Lewis puts the knife to Harvard in particular.

ALTERNATE STRATEGIES

If you remain determined to hurl yourself into the maw of the college prestige monster, there are some strategies that merit your consideration:

Go far (as in far away) – There's an old saying: "Familiarity breeds contempt." In other words, what's nearby is considered normal and everyday and so is undervalued and overlooked. This might apply to you. In the Northeast, you can't walk five yards without bumping into a boarding school student. Northeast colleges want to look elsewhere. Some kid from Two Dot, Montana may look interesting to a college AO knee deep in Exonians. And by the way, if you happen to be from Two Dot but go to Exeter, guess what? You will probably be considered a Northeast prepster, not a Montanan. One solution here is to look elsewhere. Boarding school students in California may have more overall appeal to colleges in D.C. or Boston than in-state. Those in Illinois might fare better at Dartmouth than at Northwestern. Quite a few students from U.S. boarding schools attend elite universities abroad.

Wait and Transfer – This is an old prep strategy. If you don't get into the college you want, go to the college that takes you, bear down, ace your classes, create an awesome GPA to demonstrate your academic chops, and then apply to transfer to a college similar to the one you wanted in the first place. "Well", you might say, "in that case, why shouldn't I just re-apply for transfer to my original first choice?" The answer is that colleges keep applicant files for several years. If you go back to a college that rejected you, the admission office will dig out your old file, look at the reasons why they turned you down and, most likely, will turn you down again. If you were on the wait list and on the bubble to being an admit, a stellar record at your current college might tip the balance in your favor. Also, you might manage a transfer to your original top choice college if you happen to be a "deep" legacy and/or a development case; in such circumstances, the college might find a way to quietly slip you in. (Note that some elite colleges state that they do not accept transfers except in cases when the applicant is seeking a particular program available at that college but nowhere else.)

Grad/Professional School - Spending one's undergraduate years at an Ivy college might make for amusing cocktail chatter, but the truth is that once you hit the work world, where you went for college as an undergraduate fades from importance quite quickly. Grad school does have an impact. If you plan to be an attorney and Yale shuns you for undergraduate work, you might go to your state school, save money, then apply to Yale Law School.

Your law clients might be interested in where you took your law degree; where you went before that will never come up.

The big dilemma for anyone who enjoyed their time at boarding school is this: quite likely, wherever you end up for college will be a disappointment compared to school; there's something about those teen years spent focused on learning and growing, in a close community that's solid, supportive, and steeped in tradition. Whatever that something is, college often doesn't compare in intensity. All boarding school students have lists of complaints about their schools. Once you leave yours, you may well come to miss it, despite its flaws, more than you might ever imagine.

ALUMNI LIFE

But wait! There's more...

One of the biggest surprises of boarding school is that one's education doesn't end at graduation. Over time, your student years – few in number, frozen in time like a fly in amber – will not be the totality of your school experience. Once you leave the school, your ties to it may get stronger.

Public schools have weak alumni programs; day school alumni groups are better, but none can compare to boarding school alumni associations. These are well funded and highly effective; they produce elaborate events, publications, and reunions that seek to bind fr students ever closer to the school community. Boarding alumni classes maintain close contact with their own websites, social media groups, and events; they serve as alumni and admission volunteers and as trustees and fundraisers. Most college alumni organizations pale by comparison. Only a few enjoy the kind of alumni support that boarding school grads give to their schools.

This intensity may be in evidence at commencement, but during college years, boarding school alumni, like their public and day colleagues, tend to pay scant attention to their schools. Interest tends to revive at the first major class reunion, which is held five years after graduation. This is often the time when the concept of a lifelong role as an alumna or alumnus kicks in.

Like colleges, boarding schools call on their alumni to serve as volunteers – to interview applicants, do alumni fundraising, and other tasks. Alumni events tend to become important events for families, who are often as involved in planning as the alums themselves. Service to the school and the larger community is a common alumni trait; one boarding alumnus, John F. Kennedy (Choate '35), phrased it famously, referencing a biblical maxim: "Of those to whom much is given, much is required."

These alumni relationships can be very rewarding whether your experience at school was wonderful or not. Over time, classmates you never knew (or knew but never liked) may turn into wonderful friends. As the years pass, childhood friends may lose touch, so too may family members. Fewer and fewer people will know you from way back when. While others in your life may fade away, your class and your school still stand together, one of the few enduring communities in our atomized modern world. When you return to campus for alumni events, part of your personal history will still be there, and the new students (who will seem younger and younger as the years roll by) will be part of your community, "one of us", for the rest of your life. This is the secret gift of a boarding school education: when you take that long walk to receive your diploma, you also inherit a living, enduring history.

AFTERWORD

We have now reached the end of this book, which is for you, I hope, the start of a new journey. "To make an end is to make a beginning," wrote T. S. Eliot; "The end is where we start from."

The rewards of a boarding school education can be many – intensive academics, a lively campus community, a wide array of new interests to explore, personal growth, and lifelong friendships. Such an education is not for every student or every family circumstance, but for those who embrace its challenges, a boarding school education can be a rich, even profound experience, one which may prepare you for more than what you have expected. Not for college admission alone, but college success. Not college only, but your life itself. Not your life alone, but your place in the lives of others and the world at large.

We have circled you 'round this boarding school world, which, as I hope you have come to understand, is nonlinear, relational rather than directional. This path began with a brace of basic questions: "who are you?" and "what are you looking for?" These questions are essential at the school admission stage. They reappear again when you arrive on campus. They return when you apply to college. When you go forth into the world, they arise again, but by then, you will likely be better prepared to answer them. This is your journey. With the help of your school community: your teachers and advisors, your fellow students, and the values and traditions of those who came before, you will be led forth (this is the original meaning of education, from the Latin "educare", "to lead forth") towards your true self and your place in the world. An education such as this is a treasure and a privilege. What will you do with this opportunity?

Your journey awaits. Travel well!

ACKNOWLEDGMENTS

The writing of this book has been a thorough pleasure and greatly enhanced by the wisdom and insights of many others. Ian Gracey, Dean of Admission, the Groton School, and Tom Sheppard, Dean of Enrollment Management , the Lawrenceville School, gave me wonderfully detailed notes and challenged my thinking in several areas; I am very grateful for their generosity and kindness. This project was also helped along the way by Blake Eldridge, Dean of Student Life, and Sara Tucker, Director of Financial Aid, also of the Lawrenceville School; Pete Upham, Executive Director of the Association of Boarding Schools (TABS), Richard Phelps, the TABS Director of Research and Strategic Resources; Erin Pihlaja, Head of Communications of the Emma Willard School, and her assistant Amoreena O'Bryan; and Victor L. Wright, trustee, alumnus, and parent, Deerfield Academy. I extend my sincere thanks to all of them.

Conversations with other parents have helped me to articulate some illusive emotional aspects of the boarding school experience. I am grateful to boarding school parents Diego Munoz and Adriana Vasquez de Munoz (Deerfield and Choate); Peter Polhemus (Exeter); Jesus and Lia Pena (Saint Timothy's); Fritz Cammerzell (Lawrenceville); Carlos Williamson (Saint Paul's and Deerfield); Andy Coburn, (Exeter) and Lisa Cloughen (Portsmouth Abbey and Lawrenceville). Their input has aided this book in ways both important and subtle.

My experience with Mango Publishing has been a delight from the start. My sincere thanks go to Chris McKenney for green-lighting this project, to Brenda Knight for her editorial expertise, and to Michelle Lewy for her marketing and sales guidance.

Thanks also to Hugo Villabona for his steady project management to Elina Diaz for her book design and to Natalia, Joshua, and Roberto for excellent support.

Lastly, I want to acknowledge my family: my heartfelt thanks to my mother-in-law, Judith Gutierrez de Gonzalez, in whose home the first draft of this book was written, and to my dazzling daughters, whose journeys through education helped bring this project into being: Bianca Mangravite was particularly helpful regarding school selection, campus tours, and school support systems; Francesca Mangravite brought me up to speed on student social media usage. Most of all, I extend my deepest gratitude to my wife, Sandra Gonzalez de Mangravite, whose love and encouragement were essential to the writing of *American Prep*.

RDM 2017

APPENDIX A: RESOURCES

TEST WEBSITES

Secondary School Admissions Test (SSAT) www.ssat.org
the principle entrance examination for boarding schools.

Independent School Entrance Examination (ISSE) www.erblearn.org
the principle entrance examination for private day schools

FINANCIAL AID

SSS by NAIS www.sssbynais.org
NAIS administers the SSS standard financial aid application form used
by boarding schools.

FINANCIAL AID FOR URMS

A Better Chance www.abetterchance.org

Prep for Prep www.prepforprep.org

New Jersey SEEDS www.njseeds.org

SCHOLARSHIPS

Caroline D Bradley Scholarship www.educationaladvancement.org

Jack Kent Cooke Scholarships www.jkcf.org

STANDARD APPLICATION SITES

(Note – none of these sites handles all American boarding schools)

Gateway to Prep Schools www.gatewaytoprepschools.com

TABS – The Association of Boarding Schools www.boardingschools.com

Secondary School Admissions Test (SSAT) www.ssat.org

PREP/BOARDING ORGANIZATIONS

The Association of Boarding Schools (TABS) www.boardingschools.com Hundreds of American prep schools are easily accessed here, with a wealth of supporting information

International Association of Educational Consultants (IECA): www. iecaonline.com The go-to place to find a qualified admission advisor

The National Association of independent Schools (NAIS) www.nais.org is the umbrella organization for over a thousand private nonprofit K-12 schools (boarding and day schools) in the United States.

The Ten Schools Admission Organization (TSAO). www.tenschools.org

Catholic Boarding Schools Association www.cbsa.org

Junior Boarding School Association www.jbsa.org

National Coalition of Girls Schools (NCGS) www.ncgs.org
Association of Independent Schools in New England www.aisne.org

Boarding Schools Association (UK) www.boarding.org.uk

Association of Military Colleges and Schools of the United States www.amcsus.org

NYBS: New York Boarding Schools www.nybs.org

SBSA: Small Boarding School Association www.smallboardingschools.org

SABS: Southeastern Association of Boarding Schools www.sabs.org

Western Boarding Schools Association www.wbsa.net

SCHOOL SEARCHES

Boarding School Review www.boardingschoolreview.com

Admissions Quest www.admissionsquest.com

Great Schools www.greatschools.org
www.privateschools.com

Prep Review www.prepreview.com
This site has free and fee based information, including reviews of
schools by recent alums

Niche www.niche.com
Provides search information for schools and colleges, plus nonscientific
rankings based on user surveys

ONLINE COMMUNITIES

College Confidential www.collegeconfidential.com maintains a Prep
School Admission chat board within the site's Forum section

Adventures in Boarding School
www.adventuresinboardingschool.tumblr.com
is an online community for boarding school students worldwide

LEARNING ISSUES:

Americans with Disabilities Act: www.ada.gov

Attention Deficit Disorder Association www.add.org

National Resource Center for ADHD www.chadd.org

Smart Kids with Learning Disabilities www.smartkidswithld.org

STUDY GUIDES AND AIDS

www.7SpeedReading.com

www.studyblue

www.aleks.com

www.khanacademy.org

www.ixl.com

www.quizlet.com

www.rescuetime.com time management software (fee based)

SUMMER OPPORTUNITIES

University of Pennsylvania Wharton School Pre-College Business Program www.wharton.upenn.edu/pre-college-programs/

Yale University Young Global Scholars www.globalscholars.yale.edu

TASP Telluride Association Summer Program for high school juniors www.tellurideassociation.org

The Road Less Travelled summer travel programs www.theroadlesstravelled.com

APPENDIX B: REFERENCES

BOOKS

Nelson W. Aldrich, Jr. *Old Money*. New York: Alfred A. Knopf 1988
ISBN: 0-394-57036-7

Lisa Birnbach. *The Official Preppy Handbook*. New York: Workman
Publishing 1981 ISBN: 0-89480-140-6

Frank Bruni. *Where You Go Is Not Who You Will Be*. New York: Grand
Central Publishing 2015

Benedict Carey. *How We Learn*. New York: Random House 2014
ISBN: 978-0-8129-8429-3

Peter W. Cookson, Jr. and Caroline Hodges Persell. *Preparing for Power*.
New York: Basic Books 1985 ISBN: 0-465-06268-7

William Deresiewicz. *Excellent Sheep*. New York: Free Press/Simon &
Schuster 2014 ISBN: 978-1-4767-0271-1; ISBN: 978-1-4767-0272-8; ISBN
978-1-4767-0273-5

Ross Douthat. *Privilege*. New York: Hyperion 2005 ISBN: 1-4013-0112-6

Malcolm Gladwell. *David & Goliath*. New York: Little, Brown and
Company 2013 ISBN: 9780-316-20436-1 (hc); 978-0-316-25178-5 (intl);
978-0-316-23985-1 (p)

Daniel Golden. *The Price of Admission*. New York: Crown Publishers 2006
ISBN -10: 1-4000-9796-7; ISBN -13: 978-1-4000-9796-8

Jerome Karabel. *The Chosen*. New York: Houghton Mifflin 2005
ISBN-13: 978-0-618-57458-2; ISBN-10: 0-618-57458-1

Harry R. Lewis' *Excellence without a Soul*. (2006). Philadelphia: Public
Affairs/Perseus 2006 ISBN-13: 9781-58648-501-6; 10-1-58648-501-6

Justin Muchnik. *Boarding School Survival Guide*. Albany NY: Peterson's
2014 ISBN: 978-0-7689-3873-9

Private Secondary Schools.: Petersons. Revised yearly

Arthur G. Powell. *Lessons from Privilege*. Cambridge MA: Harvard
University Press 1996 ISBN: 0-674-52549-3

Paul Tough. *How Children Succeed*. New York: Houghton Mifflin Harcourt
Publishing 2012 ISBN 978-0-547-56465-4

ARTICLES

Nelson W. Aldrich, Jr. "Preppies: The Last Upper Class?" 1979: *Atlantic
Monthly*, January issue

"Coming to America: the need for greater diversification in international
enrolment". 2016: ICEF *Monitor*, May issue

Kate Davidson. "Employers Find Soft Skills Like Critical Thinking In
Short Supply". 2016: *Wall Street Journal*, Aug 30 http://www.wsj.com/
articles/employers-find-soft-skills-like-critical-thinking-in-short-
supply-1472549400

Kate Davidson. "The Soft Skills Employers are Looking For". 2016: Wall
Street Journal, August 30 http://blogs.wsj.com/economics/2016/08/30/
the-soft-skills-employers-are-looking-for

INDEX OF SCHOOLS

(Note: This is __not__ is a comprehensive index of all American boarding schools; this is an index of the schools cited in this book)

Admiral Farragut Academy (FL), 132, 312

Andover (See Phillips Academy), 26-28, 34, 130, 146, 157, 198, 312

Annie Wright Schools (WA), 131

Avon Old Farms Schools (CT), 131

Berkshire School (MA), 27, 130, 312

Blair Academy (NJ), 130, 312

Bridgton Academy (ME), 133, 312

Brooks School (MA), 130, 312

Buxton School (MA), 29

Canterbury School (CT), 29

Carson Long Military Academy (PA), 26, 312

Cate School (CA), 27, 129, 312

Chaminade College Preparatory School (MO), 46

Cheshire Academy (CT), 133, 312

Choate Rosemary Hall (CT), 5, 129, 198, 312

Concord Academy (MA), 130, 312

Culver Academies (IN), 5, 132, 312

Dana Hall School (MA), 30

Deerfield Academy (MA), 129, 304, 312

Dunn School (CA), 132, 312

Eaglebrook School (MA), 133

Emma Willard School (NY), 26, 220, 304, 312

Episcopal High School (VA), 26, 312

Exeter (See Phillips Exeter Academy) 26, 28-29, 34, 49, 111, 130, 146, 157, 198, 297, 304, 312-313

Fay School (MA), 133

Fessenden (MA), 133, 312

Forman School (CT), 132, 312

Foxcroft Academy (ME), 131

Fryeburg Academy (ME), 26

George School (PA), 27, 34, 130, 315

Georgetown Preparatory School (MD), 26, 130, 312

Governor's Academy (MA), 26, 130

Groton School (MA), 4, 27, 130, 304

The Gunnery (CT), 26

Hill School (PA), 26, 130, 132, 312

Hockaday School (TX), 130, 312

Hotchkiss School (CT), 27, 130, 312

Hun School of Princeton (NJ), 46, 132, 312

Idyllwild Arts Academy (CA), 132, 312

Interlochen Arts Academy (MI), 132, 312

Kent School (CT), 27, 312

King's Academy (TN), 313

Lawrence Academy (MA), 26

Lawrenceville School (NJ), 4, 26, 46, 130, 304, 313, 317

Lincoln Academy (ME), 26

Linden Hall (PA), 26, 313

Loomis Chaffee (CT), 130, 146, 313

Madeira School (VA), 30

Mercersburg Academy (PA), 27, 313

Middlesex School (MA), 27, 130, 313

Milton Academy (MA), 130, 313

Miss Porter's School (CT), 26

Noble & Greenough School (MA), 130, 313
North Central Texas Academy (TX), 198, 313
Northfield Mount Hermon School (MA), 30, 146, 314

Ojai Valley School (CA), 133, 313

Peddie School (NJ), 130
Pennington School (NJ), 132, 313
Phelps School (PA), 131, 313
Phillips Academy (MA), 26, 34, 130, 313
Phillips Exeter Academy (NH), 34, 130, 313
Pomfret School (CT), 27, 313
Portsmouth Abbey School (RI), 5, 313
Proctor Academy (NH), 132, 313
Purnell School (NJ), 132
Putney School (VT), 29

Salem Academy (NC), 26
Salisbury School (CT), 131
San Marcos Academy (TX), 132, 313
Southwestern Academy (CA), 133, 313
St. Andrew's Academy (DE), 130
St. Catherine's Academy (CA), 132
St. George's School (RI), 130
St. John's Military School (KS), 132
St. Margaret's School (VA), 131
St. Mark's School (MA), 27
St. Paul's School (NH), 27, 111, 130
St. Thomas More School (CT), 133, 313
St. Timothy's School (MD), 4, 131
Suffield Academy (CT), 130, 313

Tabor Academy (MA), 27, 313

Taft School (CT), 27, 130, 313

Tallulah Falls School (GA), 198

Thacher School (CA), 5, 27, 130

THINK Global School (NY), 130

Tilton School (NY), 132

Trinity Pawling School (NY), 27

Valley Forge Military Academy (PA), 132

Vanguard School (FL), 132

Walnut Hill School (MA), 132

Washington Academy (ME), t26, 131

Webb Schools (TN), 34

Webb Schools (CA), 34

Wentworth Military Academy (MO), 198

Western Reserve Academy (OH), 26

Westminster School (CT), 27, 130

West Nottingham Academy (MD), 26

Woodberry Forest School (VA), 27

BIOGRAPHY

Award winning writer/critic **Ronald Mangravite** has multiple perspectives on the American prep school world. An alumnus of the Lawrenceville School, he is a current prep school parent, an alumni class officer, and an admissions volunteer. His teaching experience includes universities and private schools, with service on admissions and curricula committees. He holds degrees from the University of California, Berkeley and the University of California, Los Angeles.

Printed in the USA
CPSIA information can be obtained
at www.ICGtesting.com
JSHW031703140824
68134JS00036B/3500

9 781633 534896